FROM THE ★

FARM HOUSE KITCHEN

DAWN STOLTZFUS
& CAROL FALB

HARVEST HOUSE PUBLISHERS
EUGENE, OREGON

Cover by Dugan Design Group

Cover Image © dulezidar / iStock; tycoon101 / Fotolia

All oven temperatures are given in degrees Fahrenheit.

FROM THE FARMHOUSE KITCHEN

Copyright © 2018 by Dawn Stoltzfus and Carol Falb
Published by Harvest House Publishers
Eugene, Oregon 97402
www.harvesthousepublishers.com

ISBN 978-0-7369-7166-9 (pbk.)
ISBN 978-0-7369-7167-6 (eBook)

Library of Congress Cataloging-in-Publication Data

Names: Stoltzfus, Dawn, author. | Falb, Carol, author.
Title: From the farmhouse kitchen / Dawn Stoltzfus and Carol Falb.
Description: Eugene, Oregon : Harvest House Publishers, [2018]
Identifiers: LCCN 2017025492| ISBN 9780736971669 (pbk.) | ISBN 9780736971676
(ebook)
Subjects: LCSH: Cooking, American. | Farm life. | LCGFT: Cookbooks.
Classification: LCC TX715 .S872 2018 | DDC 641.5973--dc23 LC record available at
https://lccn.loc.gov/2017025492

Printed in China

17 18 19 20 21 22 23 24 25 / RDS-SK / 10 9 8 7 6 5 4 3 2 1

CONTENTS

THE ESSENCE OF FARM-TO-TABLE

Farm-to-table is all the rage right now, but what, exactly, does it mean? I (Dawn) don't proclaim myself to be *the* authority on the subject, but I did grow up on a farm. We ate beef from our own cows, which we raised and had cut and packaged for us. We drank raw milk from our own dairy herd. We raised our own vegetables and chickens. (And during the times when we didn't have chickens on the farm, we bought eggs from our Amish neighbors down the road.) We enjoyed fresh strawberries in abundance. We bought up to 100 quarts at a time so that we could mash, sweeten, and freeze some for the winter months ahead. (They still had that just-picked taste even after emerging from the freezer.)

For our family, farm-to-table was hard, hard work, but so very rewarding. Today, farm-to-table looks different from those early years. We don't live on a 100-acre farm anymore. My husband and I have 3.25 acres now, but we've been able to do a lot with what we have. We raise chickens. We don't butcher them for meat, but we do enjoy fresh eggs. We have a garden, but it's not as grand as my mother's back in the day. We have 100 blueberry and blackberry plants we grow organically, and we sell the berries to local markets.

We still enjoy raw milk from a cow share we have invested in. Our beef comes from a local grass-fed farm. We buy bushels of apples that are seconds from a local orchard. (If you have an orchard nearby, give them a call and ask what they sell on the cheap.) We support local farmers markets, and our kids love visiting them with us. In small ways, we still live farm-to-table, even though we live closer to the city now. We do the best we can with the resources that have been entrusted to us.

To me, a farm-to-table meal is…

- Fresh cucumbers and tomatoes, either in a salad or by themselves

- Sweet corn

- Sausage with green beans

- Fresh melons

- New potatoes with fresh parsley and salt and pepper. (There is nothing like fresh potatoes from our garden. We till our soil and place the seed potatoes on top of the soil. Then we cover the seedlings with three or four inches of straw or old hay. We let the potatoes do their thing, and, when it's time to harvest them, very little digging, aka *hard work*, is required. I can go out to the garden, pull back the straw, and get just enough potatoes for the night's dinner. So fun!)

My mother, Carol Falb, and I hope this book, over time, will have personal meaning for you. We pray that as you cook, as you serve, and as you make memories, you will experience little personal reminders of the Father's love toward you.

At home, our meals are simple. Homeschooling three children and chasing after a toddler has forced me to rethink meals. I love to be in the kitchen, creating, but I'm trying to accept the demands this season of life places on me. Hence, I am looking for quick and easy meals that are also healthful, fresh, and filling. If you are looking for the same thing, this is the cookbook for you.

Preparing a meal for people is one way to share God's love. My mom and I encourage you to reflect this love to the people in your sphere of influence. Speaking blessings and life over people is part of the very nature God has imparted to us as His life-giving agents. This role may not feel natural at first. It rarely does. But when we walk in His way, it becomes a more comfortable way of life. Never miss an opportunity to pray for someone who asks you to do that. And if you cannot be there in person, text or email your prayer. Prayer mysteriously centers us and pulls us toward peace and kindness.

Dawn Stoltzfus and Carol Falb

SPRING

MAIN DISHES

Asparagus, Peas, and Pasta ✂

Blackened Chicken or Salmon ✂

✣ Curried Chicken Salad

Curry Honey-Baked Chicken ✂

Deep Dish Pizza ✂

✣ Poor Man's Steak

✣ Sausage and Egg Crustless Quiche Casserole

✣ Sausage and Cheese Quiche

Sunday Chicken ✂

SAUCES, SIDE DISHES, AND SALADS

✣ Butterhorns

✣ Broccoli Salad

Caramelized Onion Dip ✂

✣ Dill Weed Egg Salad

Dipping Herbs ✂

✣ Easy Herb Butter Bread Sticks

✣ Herb Bread

Kale Apple Salad with Apple Cider Vinaigrette Dressing ✂

✣ Red and Green Salad

Roasted Asparagus with Garlic ✂

Dawn's recipes are marked with a ✂, and Carol's with a ✣.

SNACKS AND DESSERTS

Blueberry Muffins

Chocolate Whipped Cream Cake with
Chocolate-Covered Strawberries

Fruit Kabobs with Whipping Cream Dip

Fruited Tapioca

Homemade Snickers Bars

Ooey-Gooey Granola Bars

Rhubarb Crisp

Rhubarb Custard

Soft Pretzels

White Chocolate Raspberry Mousse

Dawn's recipes are marked with a , and Carol's with a .

God, in His wisdom, created seasons. We can push against them or we can press into what the season wants to give us.

Spring has a beauty all its own. Something breaks forth in our hearts in this season as we watch the virgin greens and the pastel pinks and whites take shape upon the once-barren trees. It's a season to allow new things to be born in our hearts.

ASPARAGUS, PEAS, AND PASTA

This dish is so enjoyable in the spring when fresh asparagus and peas are abundant. Whether you visit a farmer's market, grow your own, or buy frozen veggies at your grocery store, you'll have fun prepping this springtime dish. We have a pitiful asparagus patch that has struggled to produce over the past five years. (We planted our asparagus in the wrong place, and we simply haven't gotten around to moving it.) Our patch doesn't produce enough asparagus to feed our entire family for even one meal, but there's usually enough to add to a pasta dish like this one.

This is such a pretty springtime dish! There is something about the color of fresh greens. It's invigorating, reminding us that life is springing forth!

2 cups chicken broth	2 heaping cups asparagus, about 12 oz.
2 cups water	1 cup half-and-half
1 (13.25 oz.) box pasta	2 to 3 garlic cloves, minced
1 cup peas (if you use frozen peas, add two minutes of cooking time)	Salt and pepper to taste
	¼ cup Parmesan cheese, shredded

Bring the chicken broth and water to a boil. While the liquid is heating, wash the asparagus and snap into 1-inch pieces (I use only the stalks that snap easily). Once the broth and water mixture is boiling, add the pasta and cook according to package directions. At the halfway mark, add the peas. Wait 2 minutes and then add the asparagus. Remove from heat and drain in a strainer. Return to the cooking pot and add the half-and-half, garlic, salt, and pepper, and Parmesan cheese.

Serves 6 to 8

HOMESTYLE HINT

If you have fired up your grill for the spring/summer cooking season, this dish is fabulous with chicken marinated in Italian dressing. Marinate for eight hours before grilling.

BLACKENED CHICKEN OR SALMON

 When spring arrives, throw open your windows and let these smells waft from your kitchen.

SPICE MIXTURE

2 T. paprika

1 T. garlic powder

2 tsp. sea salt

1 tsp. cayenne pepper (add more pepper if you want extra heat)

1 tsp. thyme

1 tsp. basil

1 tsp. oregano

½ tsp. black pepper

MEAT PREPARATION

3 to 4 lbs. chicken breasts or salmon fillets

¼ cup butter, melted

Mix the paprika, garlic powder, salt, cayenne, thyme, basil, oregano, and black pepper in a small bowl. Place the meat on a parchment-lined baking sheet (for easy cleanup). Drizzle half of the butter over the meat. With your fingertips or a small spoon, sprinkle half of the spice mixture over the meat. Flip pieces of meat over and drizzle with the remaining butter and spices.

Heat a skillet (we like cast iron for recipes like this) to medium-high. Allow at least 4 minutes so that your pan will be good and hot. If you have leftover butter, place a bit in the hot pan and fry the meat for approximately 6 minutes. Flip and cook the other side. (Frying times will vary based on thickness of your chicken or salmon, but it should be 6 to 10 minutes per side.) You can also fry the meat for 3 minutes per side and then finish by baking in a 350° oven until fully cooked.

Serves 8 to 10

CURRIED CHICKEN SALAD

I enjoy hosting women in my home and garden. When I do, I like to keep my entrées simple. This is one of my favorite go-to recipes. I serve this chicken salad on either ready-made croissants I pick up at the grocery or a bed of lettuce with a side of sliced cantaloupe and clusters of grapes.

1 boneless, skinless chicken breast, diced (or 2 cups of leftover cooked chicken)

¼ tsp. curry powder

2 tsp. soy sauce

2 tsp. lemon juice

¾ cup mayonnaise

¾ cup red grapes, sliced

¼ cup slivered almonds

Cook the chicken breast in 1 cup water or broth until tender (or use the 2 cups of leftover chicken).

In a small bowl, mix together the curry powder, soy sauce, lemon juice, and mayonnaise. In a separate bowl, combine the grapes, almonds, and chicken. Add the dressing. Chill for several hours. Serve on lettuce, bread, or crackers.

Serves 6

CURRY HONEY-BAKED CHICKEN

This is an excellent dish to serve when expecting guests. You can easily put two chickens in a large roasting pan and prepare them together. Drizzle the pan drippings over cooked rice, and you have a glorious side dish. Just add a salad, and you have a complete meal—without spending a whole day in the kitchen. Don't you just love a main dish that is quick and easy, but also tastes so rich?

    1 whole chicken
    ¼ cup (½ stick) butter, melted
    ¼ cup honey
    1 tsp. salt
    2 tsp. curry powder

Place the chicken in a roasting pan, breast down. Mix the butter, honey, salt, and curry powder and use to season the chicken. Bake covered at 375° for 60 to 70 minutes. Remove the cover, baste with the pan drippings, and bake an additional 15 minutes.

Serves 4 to 6

DEEP DISH PIZZA

 This is a gluten-free and low-carb recipe.

1½ lbs. bulk sausage

1 large onion, chopped

1 bell pepper, chopped

8 oz. fresh mushrooms, sliced

3 eggs

1 cup almond flour

½ tsp. baking powder

¼ tsp. salt (optional)

1 cup tomato sauce

2 tsp. garlic powder

1 T. dried basil

1 tsp. oregano

2 cups mozzarella cheese, shredded

Sliced olives

Pepperoni or crumbled bacon, cooked

Red pepper flakes and additional dried basil (optional)

Preheat the oven to 400°. Fry the sausage, and when it is almost fully cooked, add the onions, bell peppers, and mushrooms. Sauté to your liking.

In a small bowl, combine the eggs, almond flour, baking powder, and salt. Grease a 9 x 13-inch pan and spread in the egg mixture. (It will barely cover the bottom of the pan.) Next, combine the tomato sauce, garlic powder, basil, and oregano. Spread gently over the egg mixture. Place the sausage mixture on top. Sprinkle mozzarella cheese on over that, and then add the olives and pepperoni or bacon. Bake for 15 to 18 minutes or until the cheese is bubbly. Remove from heat and dust with red pepper flakes and/or basil if desired.

Serves 15

POOR MAN'S STEAK

This recipe probably says love to my family more than any other. It's one of those no-fail dishes, and I always receive raves of delight when they know it's on the menu. "Poor Man's Steak" was often chosen by the birthday child when asked what he or she would like to have for dinner. It's also a good do-ahead dish to make and bake later.

3 lbs. ground beef

1 cup water

3 tsp. salt, scant

1 cup cracker crumbs

Flour for dredging

Butter for browning

1 (10.5 oz.) can cream of mushroom soup

Mix the ground beef, water, salt, and cracker crumbs together and pat into a baking sheet with sides. Refrigerate several hours or overnight.

Cut the chilled mixture into squares, dredge in flour, and then brown in melted butter on both sides. Place in a 4-quart baking dish.

Pour a little water into the browning drippings and add the mushroom soup. Stir and then pour over the browned meat. Bake at 350° for 1 hour.

Serves 10 to 15

HOMESTYLE HINT

I like to add extra mushrooms—either canned or fresh sliced—before baking.

SAUSAGE AND EGG CRUSTLESS QUICHE CASSEROLE

2 lbs. pork sausage

2 cups cheddar cheese, shredded

12 eggs, lightly beaten

4 cups milk

½ cup cream

1½ tsp. salt

1 tsp. prepared mustard

½ tsp. black pepper

2 tsp. Italian seasoning or chives

Fry the sausage and then place it in a 9 x 13-inch pan. Sprinkle the cheese over it.

In a separate bowl, combine the eggs, milk, cream, salt, mustard, black pepper, and Italian seasoning or chives. Pour over sausage and cheese mixture. Bake uncovered at 350° for 45 minutes.

Serves 12

SAUSAGE AND CHEESE QUICHE

1 lb. pork sausage

½ cup onion, chopped

1 clove garlic, minced

1 T. butter

3 eggs, beaten

1½ cups evaporated milk

1½ cups cheddar cheese, shredded

2 T. flour

¾ tsp. salt

½ tsp. ground pepper

1 8-inch pie shell

Preheat the oven to 350°. Brown the sausage, drain the grease, and put the meat in a bowl.

Sauté the onion and garlic in the butter for about 2 minutes, and then add it to the cooked sausage. Combine the rest of the ingredients and mix well. Pour the sausage mixture into the pie shell and bake for 35 minutes or until set.

Serves 6 to 8

SUNDAY CHICKEN

This is one of our families' all-time favorite meals. It's wonderful and quick, yet so, so tasty! It's amazing served with rice, using the pan juices as a drizzle over the rice.

5 lbs. bone-in chicken pieces

6 T. butter (cut into slivers and placed on top of the chicken)

2 T. Worcestershire sauce

2 T. vinegar

1 (.7 oz.) pkg. Italian salad dressing mix (we like Good Seasonings brand)

Place the chicken pieces in a 9 x 13-inch baking pan. Top with the butter. Drizzle the Worcestershire sauce and vinegar over chicken. Sprinkle on the dressing mix. Cover tightly with foil and bake for 90 minutes at 375°. If desired, remove the foil for the last 15 minutes of cooking time to brown the chicken.

Serves 6 to 7

BUTTERHORNS

1 pkg. dry yeast

2 T. warm water

2 cups warm milk

½ cup sugar

1 egg, beaten

1½ tsp. salt

6 cups flour

¾ cup (1½ sticks) butter, melted

Preheat the oven to 350°. In a large bowl, dissolve the yeast in the warm water. Add the milk, sugar, egg, salt, and 3 cups of the flour. Stir. Add the remaining flour and combine until mixed. (Do not knead.) Place the mixture into a greased bowl. Cover and refrigerate overnight.

The next day, punch down the dough and divide it in half. On a floured surface, roll each half into a 12-inch circle and cut the dough with a pizza cutter into 12 wedges. Roll each wedge, beginning with the wide end. Place the rolls, point side down, onto a baking sheet.

Cover and let rise until doubled, about 1 hour. Bake for 15 to 20 minutes. Brush the tops with the melted butter.

Makes 24 butterhorns

BROCCOLI SALAD

This is an old family recipe, and it happens to be our youngest son's favorite. After all these years, I still enjoy making it. And eating it!

1 head broccoli
1 head cauliflower
1 small onion, diced
1 lb. bacon, fried and crumbled
2 cups Hellmann's mayonnaise
¼ cup (scant) sugar
2 cups cheddar cheese, shredded

Cut the broccoli and cauliflower into small pieces. Toss these vegetables together with the diced onion and bacon crumbles. In a separate bowl, combine the mayonnaise with the sugar, and then stir that into the vegetable mixture. Add the shredded cheese just before serving and mix well once more.

Serves 12 to 14

CARAMELIZED ONION DIP

This is one of my favorite dips. I love the taste of caramelized onions in anything. We were hosting a party one night, and I wanted something different but quick. I thought it couldn't hurt to try caramelizing onions for a dip. The onions came through on this one!

2 T. butter

2 cups onion, diced small

¾ cup sour cream or plain Greek yogurt

1 cup mayonnaise

1 tsp. parsley, dried

1 tsp. seasoning salt

Melt the butter in a large skillet over medium-high heat. Add the onion and sauté for 2 to 3 minutes. Turn the heat to low and cook for 25 minutes, stirring every 5 minutes so that the onions don't burn. Allow to cool a bit.

Combine the sour cream or yogurt, mayonnaise, parsley, and salt together in a bowl. Mix in the cooled, sautéed onion and serve with a variety of vegetables or potato chips.

Serves 14 to 16

DILL WEED EGG SALAD

In spring, summer, and fall, I enjoy entertaining friends and family in my backyard. When the weather is nice, we can enjoy the outdoors and the gardens. This recipe is one I use frequently on such days. It's very simple, but the dill weed makes it seem special. I recommend serving this egg salad on multigrain or pumpernickel bread.

12 eggs

4 T. mayonnaise

1 T. prepared mustard

1½ tsp. dill weed

Salt and pepper to taste

12 slices of multigrain or pumpernickel bread

Place the eggs in a large kettle, cover with water, and bring to a boil. Boil for 10 minutes. Cool the eggs under cold water and then peel them and shred with a cheese shredder or an egg slicer. Place eggs and remaining ingredients, minus the bread, into a large bowl and mash together (a fork works well for this task). Serve on the bread.

Yields 6 sandwiches

DIPPING HERBS

This zippy and zesty herb mixture is *so* delicious served with a variety of crusty breads or on cubed potatoes baked in the oven with a bit of butter over them.

2 T. red pepper flakes

2 T. black pepper

¼ cup basil, dried

¼ cup cumin

¼ cup granulated garlic

½ cup rosemary, dried

1 cup oregano, dried

¾ cup pretzel salt or coarse sea salt

¼ cup olive oil

In a glass container, mix the red pepper flakes, black pepper, basil, cumin, garlic, rosemary, oregano, and salt. Store until ready for use. These herbs will keep for up to one year. When ready to serve, place a tablespoon of the herbs in a shallow dish, and then pour ¼ cup of olive oil over the top. A simple French bread dipped in this mixture is delicious! These herbs are also great sprinkled over roasted potatoes.

Yields 2 cups herb mixture

HOMESTYLE HINT
You can easily halve this recipe if you don't think you will use up the herb mixture in a year.

EASY HERB BUTTER BREAD STICKS

¼ cup (½ stick) butter, softened
½ tsp. Italian seasoning
1 tsp. Parmesan cheese
3 slices sourdough bread

Preheat the oven to 400°. Combine the butter, seasoning, and cheese and spread on the bread. Cut the bread into 3 strips and place on a baking sheet, butter side up.

Bake for 10 minutes or until crispy. Serve with your favorite soup. (If you are in a hurry, toast the bread and then spread the butter and cut into strips.)

Makes 9 bread sticks

HERB BREAD

 I love serving this bread as a side to soups.

2 to 3 cloves fresh garlic

3 T. butter

1 tsp. sugar

1 pkg. yeast

1 cup warm milk

1½ tsp. salt

1½ tsp. Italian seasoning or ½ tsp. of your favorite herbs
    (my favorites are dill weed, oregano, basil, rosemary, and chives)

3 to 3½ cups flour

Preheat the oven to 350°. Sauté the garlic in the butter for approximately 1 minute. Dissolve the sugar and yeast in warm milk, cool, and then add the garlic and the remainder of the ingredients. Knead with a mixer, about 5 minutes. Let rise until double.

Punch down and let rise a second time. Shape into a loaf and place into a greased bread pan or on a baking stone and let rise again. Bake for 30 minutes.

Yields one loaf

KALE APPLE SALAD WITH APPLE CIDER VINAIGRETTE DRESSING

 I had to learn to acquire a taste for kale, but I'm glad I did. Kale is packed with things that are good for you. Here is a simple recipe for those of us who love fruit with our salads.

SALAD

6 to 8 cups kale, spines removed

1 cup sliced or slivered almonds

1 T. butter

1 apple, thinly sliced

¼ cup Craisins (or any brand of dried cranberry)

DRESSING

¼ cup onion, chopped fine

1 clove garlic, minced

3 T. apple cider vinegar

3 T. olive oil

¼ tsp. salt

¼ cup maple syrup

Wash and tear the kale into small pieces and set aside. In a small saucepan, melt the butter over low heat. Add the almonds, stirring occasionally. Toast until the almonds start to turn brown, about 5 to 7 minutes. Remove from heat.

In a small jar, add the onion, garlic, apple cider vinegar, olive oil, and salt. Cover and shake for one minute. When the ingredients are thoroughly combined, add the maple syrup and shake again. Pour half of the dressing over the kale—or all of it, if desired. Stir well and allow to sit for 20 minutes. Add the almonds, apple slices, and dried cranberries just before serving.

Serves 6

RED AND GREEN SALAD

SALAD

    5 oz. spring mix lettuces

    5 oz. red leaf lettuce

    5 oz. baby spinach

    Romano or feta cheese, for garnish

    Red onion, thinly sliced, for garnish

    Dried cranberries, for garnish

Combine the lettuces and spinach. Set aside the last three ingredients for the garnish.

RASPBERRY SALAD DRESSING

    ¼ cup oil

    1 T. raspberry vinegar

    1 tsp. lime juice

    1 tsp. sugar

    ½ tsp. salt

Place the ingredients in a blender and blend until smooth.

SPICY PECANS

    ¼ cup powdered sugar

    ½ tsp. salt

    ¼ tsp. allspice

    ⅛ tsp. nutmeg

    ⅛ tsp. cayenne pepper (optional)

    ⅓ cup pecans

Combine the sugar and spices in a small bowl. Rinse the pecans with water and drain, but do not let dry. Add the pecans to the sugar mixture and toss well. Arrange on baking sheet lined with parchment paper. Bake for 8 to 10 minutes at 350°, stirring occasionally. Along with the salad dressing, toss the pecans with the salad just before serving.

Garnish the salad with thinly shaved Romano or feta cheese, thin-sliced red onion, and dried cranberries.

Serves 6 to 8

ROASTED ASPARAGUS WITH GARLIC

1½ to 2 lbs. asparagus, washed and snapped

2 T. butter

Salt and pepper to taste

2 garlic cloves or 1 tsp. garlic, minced

Preheat the oven to 400°. Wash the asparagus and snap until you get to the hard part of the stem; discard the woody stems. Place on a baking sheet. Sliver the butter over the top and sprinkle on the salt and pepper. Bake for 8 minutes. Remove from the oven, stir, and add the garlic. Return to the oven and bake another 5 minutes or longer, depending on how you like your asparagus.

Serves 6 to 8

STRESS BUSTERS

What stresses you out when it comes to hosting? Whatever the cause of stress, there is usually a creative solution. Is it the dishes afterward? Free yourself and buy paper plates and cups and plastic utensils.

When it comes to hosting a meal, my husband, Merv, and I have learned how to respect each other's personal preferences. He knows what is important to me, and vice versa. For example, I love the small details. He sometimes thinks those details are just too much to deal with, but he doesn't make this a point of contention. Instead, he steps up and makes things happen. I, on the other hand, know he likes a swept floor, so most nights, after all the guests have gone and my family is in bed fast asleep, I will get out the little dust sweeper and make a swipe through the house. Sure, it's late and I'm tired, but these are little ways we can honor each other.

Don't we all have fears or concerns that keep us from hosting a meal? We can find ways to tackle them. Are you afraid that your meat dish won't turn out? Buy a rotisserie chicken—you can't go wrong with that. If dessert is your concern, buy one from a local bakery or restaurant. Or simply serve ice cream. Scoop it into some pretty dishes and let your guests decorate their desserts with sprinkles, syrups, and whipped cream. Most of our guests have kids, and they love this! (Meanwhile, you will have preserved your sanity.)

Above all, keep in mind that most people won't care what you served. They probably won't even remember what was on the menu. But they will remember if they felt loved and cared for while they were in your home. Be aware of their needs. If you know your guests enjoy coffee, have plenty on hand. And wear a smile, even when the kids have spilled ten cups of water. You are serving in Jesus's name. You're His agent in this moment.

Things can be chaotic when I am putting the finishing touches on preparation for a dinner party, but I pray, "Lord Jesus, please bless our guests this evening. Help us to minister to their needs, even those needs we aren't aware of." After I pray, my heart is quieted, and my soul finds rest in the knowledge that I have released my ambitions to Him. I want Him to be honored in my serving.

We have the privilege of inviting Jesus to join us as we share a meal with others. Sometimes, our guests' beautiful souls are broken, and we have the opportunity to offer them a ray of hope as we serve them. Yes, it can be tiring, but there is always tomorrow to rest.

BLUEBERRY MUFFINS

3 cups flour

4 tsp. baking powder

1 tsp. salt

1 cup sugar

2 eggs

1 cup milk

½ cup oil

½ cup plain yogurt

2 cups blueberries

Preheat the oven to 350°. In a medium-sized bowl, mix together the flour, baking powder, salt, and sugar.

In another bowl, combine the eggs, milk, oil, and yogurt. Stir this mixture into the dry ingredients until just blended. (The batter will be slightly lumpy.)

Fold in the blueberries and drop the batter into greased muffin tins. Bake for 20 to 25 minutes, being careful not to overbake.

Yields 18 muffins

CHOCOLATE WHIPPED CREAM CAKE WITH CHOCOLATE-COVERED STRAWBERRIES

My husband, Merv, is an incredibly disciplined eater, but he does enjoy an occasional dessert. It's so fun for me to create a sweet treat he really loves, and he reveres chocolate in all forms. Plus, strawberries are his favorite fruit, and he prefers a light frosting to the heavier varieties. This dessert checks all those boxes.

By the way, this recipe makes a great birthday cake. It's quick to prepare and requires very few dishes. Score!

CHOCOLATE CAKE

1 cup (2 sticks) butter

1 cup water

¼ cup + ½ tsp. cocoa powder, divided

1 cup sour cream

¼ tsp. salt

1 tsp. vanilla extract

2 cups raw or granulated sugar

1 tsp. baking soda

2 cups flour

2 eggs, lightly beaten

CHOCOLATE-COVERED STRAWBERRIES

14 to 16 strawberries, washed and dried

1 cup semisweet chocolate chips

CHOCOLATE WHIPPED CREAM FROSTING

3 cups whipping cream

⅓ cup cocoa powder

¾ cup powdered sugar

1½ tsp. vanilla extract

Preheat the oven to 350°. In a saucepan, combine the butter, water, and ¼ cup of the cocoa powder. Bring to a boil, stirring constantly. Remove from heat and add the sour cream, salt, vanilla, sugar, baking soda, flour, and eggs. Mix this cake batter thoroughly with a hand mixer (recommended). Lightly butter the bottoms and sides of two 9-inch round cake pans. Sprinkle ½ teaspoon of the cocoa powder on the pans' sides and bottoms (this will help the cakes pop easily out of the pans). Bake for 22 to 24 minutes or until an inserted toothpick comes out clean. Cool on a wire rack, turning the pans upside down (another way to ensure easy removal).

While the cake is baking (or cooling), wash the strawberries and pat dry with a paper towel. In a double boiler (or you can use a glass bowl that fits over a saucepan), melt the chocolate chips on very low heat. Dip strawberries halfway in the melted chocolate and place on wax paper to cool and harden.

When the cake is completely cool, whip the whipping cream until soft peaks form. Add the cocoa powder, powdered sugar, and vanilla. Beat just until the whipping cream holds its shape. (This takes less time than one might imagine.)

Cut both cakes in half so that you have 4 layers. Place your first layer on a pretty platter and put about one cup of the frosting on top of it. Repeat the process with each succeeding layer. Spread a layer of whipped cream on top of your cake. Next, use a cake-decorating bag (or plastic storage bag with one end cut off) to make 7 or 8 large-marshmallow-size dollops of the remaining frosting around the rim of the top layer. (I have also used a small cookie scoop to make these marshmallow-sized frosting pillows for the strawberries.) Place a chocolate-covered strawberry in the center of each dollop. Arrange the remaining strawberries in the center of the cake. Serve immediately or refrigerate until you're ready to eat. Store the uneaten cake in the refrigerator.

Serves 14 to 16

HOMESTYLE HINT

The amount of semisweet chocolate you will need may vary greatly depending on the size of your strawberries. Strawberry size fluctuates with the seasons, so you may need more (or less) chocolate to get the job done.

FRUIT KABOBS WITH WHIPPING CREAM DIP

I could swim in this stuff. It's seriously that good! I often use this dip when I want to do something special but also have it be a bit healthier for my family.

DIP

    1 cup whipping cream

    8 oz. cream cheese, room temperature

    14 oz. sweetened condensed milk

    1 tsp. vanilla

Beat the whipping cream on high until it starts to hold its shape in the bowl (about 3 to 4 minutes). In a separate bowl, beat the cream cheese until smooth. Add the sweetened condensed milk and blend. Add the whipped cream and vanilla and mix until nice and creamy. This recipe is best when served fresh or used within a couple of days because the whipped cream becomes runny.

Yields 4 cups

FRUIT

    ½ lb. grapes

    1 lb. strawberries

    4 kiwis

    Half of a fresh pineapple

    Kabob sticks (16 to 18)

Wash, clean, and cut the fruit to your liking. Thread the fruit chunks onto the sticks in whatever arrangement you desire.

Yields 16 to 18 kabobs

HOMESTYLE HINT

Don't feel that you must skewer your fruit onto kabob sticks. You can cut and serve the fruit on a platter with the dip on the side.

FRUITED TAPIOCA

This dish is such a special family recipe. It was a favorite dessert at my grandma and grandpa's house. Dawn remembers enjoying it at Sunday lunches.

5 cups water

Pinch of salt

1 cup small pearl tapioca

½ cup sugar

1 (3 oz.) box flavored gelatin (orange or raspberry)

2 cups fresh raspberries or 1 (15 oz.) can mandarin oranges, undrained

2 cups whipped cream, sweetened

Bring the water and a pinch of salt to a boil and then add the tapioca. Cook for 20 minutes or until the tapioca is clear. Add the sugar and the gelatin. Stir well and then let cool. Add the raspberries and whipped cream if using raspberry gelatin. If using orange gelatin, add the mandarin oranges and the whipped cream.

Serves 6 to 8

HOMEMADE SNICKERS BARS

If you are a Snickers fan, you'll love this homemade version of the popular candy bar. Let's just say you probably won't eat just one!

BASE LAYER

1 cup milk chocolate chips
¼ cup butterscotch chips
¼ cup creamy peanut butter

Combine these three ingredients in a small saucepan, stirring over low heat until melted and smooth. Spread onto the bottom of a lightly greased 9 x 13-inch pan. Refrigerate until set.

FILLING

¼ cup butter
1 cup sugar
¼ cup evaporated milk
1½ cups marshmallow crème
¼ cup crunchy peanut butter
1 tsp. vanilla
Chopped salted peanuts (optional)

Melt the butter in a heavy saucepan over medium-high heat. Add the sugar and milk. Bring to a boil and stir for 5 minutes. Remove from heat and stir in marshmallow crème, peanut butter, and vanilla. If you want crunchier bars, add half a cup of salted peanuts. Spread over first layer. Refrigerate until set.

CARAMEL LAYER

 1 (14 oz.) pkg. caramels
 ¼ cup whipping cream

Combine the caramels and whipping cream in a saucepan and stir over low heat until the caramels are melted and smooth. Spread over the filling. Refrigerate until set.

TOP LAYER

 1 cup milk chocolate chips
 ¼ cup butterscotch chips
 ¼ cup creamy peanut butter

In a saucepan, combine the chips and peanut butter. Stir over low heat until melted and smooth. Pour over the caramel layer. Refrigerate for at least one hour. Cut into 1-inch squares and store in a cool place.

Yields 117 squares

OOEY-GOOEY GRANOLA BARS

My children *love* Rice Krispies Treats, something inspired by their father. But letting them eat only Rice Krispies Treats gives them a sugar high because that treat is a sweet without any protein to anchor it. These granola bars, on the other hand, include peanut butter, walnuts, and chia seeds, so they are a compromise, and everyone is happy with the results. The kids get their ooey-gooey treats, and I have peace of mind knowing they are getting some protein. Another bonus: This is a quick-mix recipe with no baking required.

½ cup (1 stick) butter

20 oz. marshmallows

½ cup honey

½ cup peanut butter

1 tsp. salt

5 cups oatmeal

5 cups Rice Krispies (or other crisped-rice cereal)

1 cup chopped walnuts

¼ cup chia seeds

¾ to 1 cup mini chocolate chips (you can use fewer chips if desired)

Spray or butter a jelly roll pan. In a large kettle, melt the butter over low heat. Add the marshmallows, stirring often so the mixture doesn't burn on the bottom but the marshmallows melt (keep the heat on low). Remove from heat. Add the honey, peanut butter, and salt. Stir until completely mixed, and then stir in the oatmeal, cereal, walnuts, and chia seeds. Spread the mixture onto the jelly roll pan immediately. (If your mixture hardens too quickly, set it on the stovetop for a minute or two over low heat.) Sprinkle the chocolate chips on top and press lightly with your hands into granola mixture so they stick.

Yields 30 to 36 bars

HOMESTYLE HINT

*Wrap some of these bars in plastic wrap or waxed
paper bags and store them in your cookie jar. Granola
bars and milk make a great after-school snack.*

RHUBARB CRISP

Rhubarb is a strange sort of plant. It's one of those either "love it" or "hate it" foods. I fall in the "love it" category. I can hardly wait for it to pop up in my garden in the spring so we can taste its one-of-a-kind goodness.

FRUIT BASE

4 cups rhubarb, diced

1 cup sugar

3 T. flour

Combine the ingredients and then place the fruit mixture in an 8 x 8-inch buttered baking dish.

TOPPING

1 cup brown sugar

1 cup quick oats

1½ cups flour

¾ cup (1½ sticks) butter, softened

Preheat the oven to 375°. Mix together the brown sugar, oats, and flour and then cut in the butter. Spread over the rhubarb mixture and bake for 30 to 40 minutes.

Serves 6 to 8

RHUBARB CUSTARD

Here is another dessert for rhubarb lovers, but if you don't generally care for this sour, fruity vegetable (often used in desserts), you might try this recipe. I'll bet you'll like it.

CRUST

2 cups flour

1 cup butter

¼ cup powdered sugar

Preheat the oven to 325°. Mix the ingredients together and press into a 9 x 13-inch pan. Bake for 10 minutes. (Keep the oven on, as you'll need it again after making the custard layer.)

CUSTARD LAYER

5 cups rhubarb, cubed

2 cups sugar

3 eggs, beaten

1 cup cream or half-and-half

7 T. flour

Place the cubed rhubarb on top of the crust.

Combine the sugar, eggs, cream, and flour and pour over the rhubarb. Bake for 35 minutes.

After cooling, spread with your favorite whipped topping.

Serves 8 to 10

SOFT PRETZELS

This is a fun recipe to make with grandchildren. Allowing kids to shape their own pretzels brings out their creativity, and it makes lasting memories. Sometimes it's tempting to quickly make these by myself, as there is less mess and fuss, but then where are the memories?

As I reflect on the ages of our 13 grandchildren, I wonder how the time has passed by so quickly. They have grown from babies to teenagers in no time, and I often wonder, *Do my grandchildren have good memories of being with their grandmother?* How I pray that our loving God will redeem our times together! I am continually challenged to spend more quality time with each precious one. I can't help but think of the Gaither Vocal Band song, "We Have This Moment Today." What will I do with *my* moments?

1 T. yeast

1¼ cups warm water

¼ cup brown sugar

4 cups flour

7 tsp. baking soda, divided

4 cups water (for dipping the pretzels)

Pretzel salt

In a large bowl, dissolve the yeast in the warm water and add the brown sugar, flour, and 2 teaspoons baking soda. Mix well. Let rise for 20 minutes.

In another bowl, combine the 4 cups water and remaining 5 teaspoons baking soda. Shape the dough into pretzels and then dip them into this water mixture.

Place on a well-greased baking sheet and sprinkle with pretzel salt. Bake at 500° for 5 to 7 minutes. Brush with melted butter when baked.

Yields approximately 16 pretzels.

I SPIES

I am constantly on the lookout for what I call "I spies." These are little unexpected beauties that come my way in the form of sight, smell, taste, touch, or hearing. The neat thing about these is that they are not happenstance. I believe they are truly gifts from God to me. Gifts such as the smell of drying hay in the summer, freshly brewed coffee, or bread baking in the oven. Maybe looking out my kitchen window and seeing a pair of bluebirds sitting in the tree, chirping to each other. How about beautiful sunrises and sunsets or an unexpected flower or butterfly? And then there are the voices of grandchildren and children in my house and garden. The laughter of loved ones. These are just a few of the things that warm my heart and remind me that God loves me and speaks to me in unexpected ways.

What about you? What are your "I spies"? How does God tell *you* that you are loved?

WHITE CHOCOLATE RASPBERRY MOUSSE

2 cups whipping cream

½ cup powdered sugar

1 tsp. vanilla

1 cup white chocolate chips, melted

8 oz. cream cheese, room temperature

1¼ cups frozen red raspberries, thawed and slightly drained

Fresh mint leaves (optional)

Canned whipped cream (optional)

Beat the whipping cream until soft peaks form. Add the powdered sugar and vanilla, and continue beating until stiff peaks start to form. Set aside.

Melt the white chocolate chips over very low heat, stirring constantly. Allow white chocolate to cool to the touch. Beat the cream cheese until smooth, and then stir it into the white chocolate.

Add the whipped cream to the white chocolate mixture until just combined, and then carefully stir in the raspberries. Scoop the mousse with an ice cream scooper into pretty little soufflé dishes or into a small, clear bowl. Fresh mint and a shot of whipped cream make a pretty garnish to these little bowls of yummy!

Serves 8 to 10

HOMESTYLE HINT

Melting chocolate can be frustrating. After many failed attempts, I know that slower is better for this task. If you use a microwave, always use a very low setting. It's the same story on the stovetop. I use the lowest setting possible, and I stir constantly. If you find the chocolate starts to harden, remove it from heat immediately and keep stirring! This step is usually enough to save your chocolate

Here's another tip: Add a tablespoon of coconut oil to the chocolate (after it's mostly melted). This will give your chocolate a smooth consistency and help prevent that annoying hardening.

SUMMER

MAIN DISHES
Farmer's Breakfast
Fresh Tomato Pie
Frittatas
Hobo Dinner
Philly Steak and Green Peppers
Ranch Potatoes
Ranch Potato Casserole
Sausage Balls
Taco Salad
Turkey and Mandarin Bread Salad

SAUCES, SIDE DISHES, AND SALADS
Almond Honey Mustard Salad
Baked Spaghetti Squash
Blackberry Sauce
Caesar Salad
Crunchy Corn Chip Salad with Sweet Dressing
Fresh Pineapple Salsa
Grilled Eggplant
Marinade for BBQ Chicken
Pesto
Red Raspberry Poppy Seed Dressing
Summer Apple Salad
Stuffed Zucchini
Tuna Salad for One
Zucchini Sauté

Dawn's recipes are marked with a 🌿 , and Carol's with a 🌾 .

SNACKS AND DESSERTS

Blackberry Goodness

Chocolate Chip Cookies

Chocolate-Covered Strawberries with White Chocolate Drizzle

Easy-as-Pie Custard Pie

Fresh Strawberry or Peach Pie

Fruit Pizza

Italian Cream Soda

Lemon Raspberry Muffins

Lemon Raspberry No-Bake Cheesecake

Peach Half-Moon Pies

Red Raspberry Bars with Crumb Topping

Red Raspberry Torte

Refreshing Slush Ice Cubes

Zucchini Bread

Dawn's recipes are marked with a ✂, and Carol's with a ✿ .

S ummer gives us intense heat. It can press in on us and test us. What are we really made of? Can our hearts withstand the pressure or will we cave?

I am amazed at what can spring forth in my garden in the summer heat.

With all of the summer produce and chores, sometimes we have more work than we'd like to think about. But we find that summer calls forth discipline in our souls, and one of the fruits of that discipline is joy in a job well done. Is there a place in your soul right now where "summer heat" is pressing in? Can you stay with the discomfort and let your soul grow as you bring your worries and concerns to the Father who already knew you would walk this path?

FARMER'S BREAKFAST

This is a great recipe when serving hungry farmers or anyone with a hearty appetite. This is an easy and tasty one-dish meal!

2 lbs. bacon

1 small onion, or 1 T. minced garlic

2 lbs. frozen hash brown potatoes, thawed

10 eggs

Salt and pepper to taste

2 cups cheddar cheese, shredded
   (use 1 cup cheddar and 1 cup pepper jack cheese, if desired)

1 T. parsley

In a large skillet, fry the bacon and onion or garlic until the bacon is crisp. Drain all but a half cup of the drippings. Add the hash browns to the skillet and mix well. Cook over medium heat for 10 minutes, turning when browned. Make 10 "wells" (indentations) evenly spaced in the hash browns and crack an egg in each well. Sprinkle with salt and pepper. Cover and cook over low heat until the eggs are set. Spread the cheese over the top and allow to melt. Garnish with parsley and serve immediately.

Serves 10

FRESH TOMATO PIE

This dish provides a nice luncheon entrée or is good for brunch as well. It's a great way to use those garden-fresh tomatoes.

1 pie shell
½ lb. bulk sausage
⅓ cup Parmesan cheese
⅓ cup half-and-half
1 clove fresh garlic, minced
⅓ cup mayonnaise
1 tsp. Italian seasoning
Salt and pepper to taste
2 cups fresh tomatoes, diced (about 2 large tomatoes)
½ cup cheddar cheese, shredded

Preheat the oven to 350°. Prick the pie shell with a fork and bake for 15 minutes.

While the pie shell is baking, fry the sausage. Once it's cool, combine it with the Parmesan cheese, half-and-half, garlic, mayonnaise, and seasonings. Pour into baked pie shell and arrange the tomatoes on top.

Bake for 30 minutes. Remove from the oven and sprinkle with the cheddar cheese. Return the pie to the oven until the cheese is melted.

Serves 6 to 8

FRITTATAS

If you are a gardener and love to use your own fresh vegetables in your entrées, we have a feeling you will like this dish. This is one of those recipes that lets you use as many different veggies as you like—or even none at all if you've already reached your veggie quota for the day.

1 cup red-skinned potatoes, diced

½ cup onion, diced, or 1 tsp. garlic, minced (optional)

3 T. Italian salad dressing

1 cup mushrooms, sliced

1 cup red pepper, chopped

⅓ cup water

1½ cups cheddar cheese, divided

10 eggs, beaten

½ cup mayonnaise (we like to use Hellmann's)

½ tsp. dried oregano

½ tsp. dried basil

Preheat the oven to 375°. Combine the potatoes, onion or garlic, and salad dressing in a skillet and cook over medium heat. Sauté until browned. Add the mushrooms, red pepper, water, and any other vegetables you desire. Cover and cook just until tender. Uncover and cook until the liquid has evaporated.

Place the vegetables into a greased, round baking dish. (We love to bake frittatas in an iron skillet.) Top with half of the cheese. Whisk together the remaining ingredients, except for the other portion of cheese. Pour over first layer, then top with remaining cheese. Bake for 40 minutes. Let set for 5 minutes before serving.

Serves 6 to 8

HOMESTYLE HINT

When baking egg dishes, a good way to tell if they are done is to insert a knife into the center. If the knife comes out clean, your eggs are baked.

HOBO DINNER

This recipe is the indoor version of a family camp favorite. When our children were young, we would camp at least once a year, and the "Hobo Dinner" was our Friday night meal. At the time I don't think they all appreciated the cabbage so much, but they have since come to like it. This dish is especially good made over a campfire…but then, aren't all camp foods exceptionally good?

1 head cabbage, torn in pieces or shredded

1 lb. ground beef

4 cups potatoes, shredded

4 medium carrots, shredded

1 small onion (optional)

8 slices American or provolone cheese

4 T. butter

Salt and pepper to taste

Place a layer of cabbage in a 9 x 13-inch baking pan. Layer the rest of ingredients, except the cheese, ending with a layer of cabbage on top. Dot with butter and cover with foil. Bake at 350° for 1 hour. Remove the foil and add the cheese, allowing it to melt before serving.

Serves 12

HOMESTYLE HINT

If you're interested in the camp version, just tear aluminum foil pieces for the amount of servings you want, layer the ingredients, and tightly fold the edges together. Place the packets directly onto hot coals. Cook for about 20 minutes on each side. Add the cheese after opening the packets.

I like to serve this dish with freshly made applesauce. If you don't have applesauce, just peel and slice about six apples into a sauce pan. Add one-quarter cup water, and cook until tender. You can add sugar and ground cinnamon to taste.

PHILLY STEAK AND GREEN PEPPERS

 This is a great dish to make if you have an abundance of green peppers in your garden or refrigerator.

1 medium onion, diced

2 T. butter

8 oz. mushrooms, washed and sliced

2 garlic cloves, minced

Salt and pepper to taste

16 oz. deli roast beef, cut into strips

4 to 6 green peppers, halved and cleaned out

1½ cups mozzarella cheese, shredded

Preheat the oven to 400°. Sauté onion in butter for 5 minutes. Add the mushrooms and cook over high heat for about 2 minutes, stirring often. Then turn down the heat and sauté for a few minutes longer. (See hint below.) Remove from heat and add the garlic, salt, and pepper to the onion mixture.

Place the roast beef strips into the green pepper halves. Add a half tablespoon of the onion mixture and top with shredded cheese.

Bake for 14 to 16 minutes. The peppers will be semicrisp. If you prefer softer peppers, bake them for 8 minutes *before* filling them. After they are filled, bake for another 14 to 16 minutes.

Serves 8 to 10

HOMESTYLE HINT

I have discovered that if fresh mushrooms are stored too long, they tend to hold more moisture, so you have to sauté them longer and at a high or medium-high heat for the liquid to cook off. I dislike slimy mushrooms, so I cook them on medium-high heat until they are crispier and brown.

RANCH POTATOES

POTATO MIXTURE

 8 medium-sized potatoes (red are good, but white also work)

 ½ cup sour cream

 ½ cup ranch dressing

 ¼ cup cooked and crumbled bacon

 1 cup cheddar cheese, shredded

Preheat the oven to 350°. Wash and cut the potatoes into quarters and boil until just tender. While the potatoes are cooking, mix the sour cream, ranch dressing, bacon, and cheese.

Drain the potatoes and place into a slightly greased 9 x 13-inch baking dish. Pour the sour cream mixture over all.

TOPPING

 ¼ cup butter, melted

 2 cups cracker crumbs or cornflakes

 ½ cup cheddar cheese, shredded

Mix the ingredients together and spread over the potato mixture. Bake for 40 minutes.

Serves 12

RANCH POTATO CASSEROLE

6 to 8 medium potatoes, quartered

½ cup sour cream

½ cup ranch dressing

¼ cup bacon, cooked and crumbled

2 T. parsley

1 cup cheddar cheese, shredded

2 cups cornflakes, slightly crushed

¼ cup melted butter

Preheat the oven to 350°. Boil the potatoes until soft. When cooled, shred and set aside.

In a bowl, combine the remaining ingredients except the cornflakes and melted butter. Add the shredded potatoes and gently mix together. Place the potato mixture in a greased 9 x 13-inch baking pan. Then mix the cornflakes with the melted butter and spread over the potato mixture. Bake for 40 to 50 minutes.

Serves 12

SAUSAGE BALLS

 These savory sausage balls are great for breakfast or served as appetizers.

1 lb. pork sausage

½ cup baking mix (such as Bisquick)

½ cup cheddar cheese, shredded

1 T. parsley flakes

1 (5 oz.) jar marmalade preserves

Preheat the oven to 350°. In a fairly large bowl, combine all of the ingredients except the preserves. Mix well and form into balls. (We have found that the best way to mix and shape the sausage balls is to use your hands). Arrange on an ungreased baking sheet and bake for 25 minutes. Heat the preserves and pour over the meatballs.

Yields 18 balls

HOMESTYLE HINT

The thing we like about this recipe is that it can be made ahead and then, on the day of serving, put in a slow cooker on low until heated through.

TACO SALAD

SALAD

1 lb. hamburger, fried and drained

1 (1¼ oz.) pkg. taco seasoning, divided

1 medium head lettuce, chopped

8 oz. cheddar cheese, grated (grated baby Swiss cheese is also good)

1 (15 oz.) can dark red kidney beans

1 large onion, diced

2 medium tomatoes, diced

1 (10 oz.) pkg. Doritos, broken

Brown the hamburger, drain, and then add the taco seasoning, reserving 1 tablespoon for the dressing. Let cool and then combine it in a large bowl with the rest of the salad ingredients except the Doritos.

DRESSING

1 T. taco seasoning

8 oz. French dressing

⅓ cup sugar

8 oz. taco sauce

In a small bowl, mix all ingredients together and then add to the salad. Toss in the Doritos just before serving.

Serves 6

TURKEY AND MANDARIN BREAD SALAD

SALAD

  2 cups turkey, cut into bite-sized pieces (you can use chicken if desired)

  2 T. oil

  2 cups hearty, whole-grain bread, cubed

  1 T. extra virgin olive oil

  6 cups baby spinach

  ¼ cup mandarin oranges (or more if desired)

  ¼ cup dried cranberries

  ¼ red onion, thinly sliced

  2 oz. blue cheese

  ¼ cup walnuts

Preheat the oven to 350°. In a skillet, heat the oil and then add the turkey (or chicken if using). Cook until done and then set aside and let cool.

In medium bowl, toss the bread cubes with the olive oil and then spread in a 15 x 10-inch baking pan. Bake for 10 to 15 minutes or until lightly toasted, stirring twice.

Next, in a large salad bowl, toss the spinach, turkey (or chicken), mandarin oranges, dried cranberries, and onion, leaving out the blue cheese and walnuts to add later.

DRESSING

⅓ cup white wine vinegar

¼ cup extra virgin olive oil

1 T. Dijon mustard

¼ tsp. salt

¼ tsp. pepper

In a medium bowl, whisk together the white wine vinegar, olive oil, mustard, salt, and pepper.

Toss the warm bread pieces with the dressing. Add the bread and dressing to the salad mixture. Toss. Top with the blue cheese and walnuts.

Serves 6

ALMOND HONEY MUSTARD SALAD

1 cup slivered almonds, or sugared-and-slivered almonds, if desired

2 T. sugar

1 head romaine lettuce, cut up

4 hard-boiled eggs

1 (11 or 15 oz.) can mandarin oranges, drained

1 cup cheddar cheese, shredded

Honey mustard dressing (of your choice)

Place the slivered almonds in a large saucepan and then sprinkle the sugar over the top. Cook over medium-low heat, stirring frequently, until sugar starts to melt and coat the almonds—about 10 minutes. (You can skip this step if you are using sugared-and-slivered almonds.) Remove from heat and allow to cool. Place lettuce in a serving bowl. Peel and dice the hard-boiled eggs and place on top of lettuce. Add the oranges and cheese. When the almonds are cooled, sprinkle them on top. Serve with honey mustard dressing and enjoy.

Serves 6 to 8

BAKED SPAGHETTI SQUASH

We love pasta in our house, especially my husband. This recipe is a bit healthier and lower in carbs than traditional spaghetti. Merv still gets his pasta (sort of), and I can use a variety of our favorite sauces, such as Alfredo, pesto, or marinara.

Spaghetti squash is a fairly easy plant to raise in your garden. We plant all of our pumpkins and squash in large empty coffee cans with both ends cut off. This technique helps ward off cutworms. Wasn't it creative of God to give us spaghetti in the shell of a squash?

1 or 2 large spaghetti squashes
Parchment paper
4 T. browned butter
Salt and pepper to taste

Wash the squash, remove the stem(s), and cut in half lengthwise. Scoop out the seeds if desired. (You can bake a squash with the seeds in.) Place parchment paper on a cookie sheet and put the squash cut-side down. Bake at 400° for 1½ hours (for a medium-sized squash). Remove from the oven, turn over, and fork out your "spaghetti." Top with browned butter, salt, and pepper.

Serves 4 to 8, depending on the size of the squash (a small squash, 4 to 6; a large squash, 6 to 8)

HOMESTYLE HINT

Another easy way to bake a spaghetti squash is to wash it, poke it several times with a paring knife, and place it whole in your slow cooker. Add ½ cup water and cook on low for 5 to 6 hours. Remove the squash, place on a cutting board, and cut in half lengthwise. Scoop out the seeds. The squash will almost fall out, along with the seeds.

BLACKBERRY SAUCE

If you like to serve pancakes to your family—but sometimes tire of traditional pancake syrup—try this recipe.

½ cup sugar

1 T. cornstarch

½ cup water

2 cups blackberries

Combine the sugar and cornstarch in a saucepan. Stir in water and bring to a boil. Boil for 3 or 4 minutes, being sure to stir constantly. Add the berries. Reduce the heat and simmer for 10 minutes. Serve warm.

Yields 2 cups

CAESAR SALAD

SALAD

    1 large bunch romaine lettuce, chopped

    2 cups black olives

    ¼ red onion, thinly sliced

    1 (5 oz.) pkg. Caesar croutons

    1 medium-sized tomato, diced

    4 oz. Parmesan cheese, grated

    4 oz. Swiss cheese, grated

Toss together all ingredients.

DRESSING

    ½ cup mayonnaise

    ⅓ cup vinegar

    1 tsp. olive oil

    2 T. Karo syrup

    ¼ cup Parmesan or Romano cheese, shredded

    ½ tsp. garlic salt

    ½ tsp. Italian seasoning,

    1 T. lemon juice

Mix the dressing ingredients together and toss with salad just prior to serving.

Serves 6

CRUNCHY CORN CHIP SALAD WITH SWEET DRESSING

SALAD

1 head lettuce, chopped

6 hard-boiled eggs, peeled and diced

1 lb. bacon, fried and crumbled

1 9¼ oz. pkg. corn chips, crushed

Mix all salad ingredients except the corn chips into large salad bowl. Save the corn chips for later (see below).

DRESSING

1¼ cups mayonnaise

⅓ cup brown sugar

⅓ cup white sugar

3 T. apple cider vinegar

Mix together the dressing ingredients, and just before serving, pour dressing over your salad and mix well. Add the corn chips and mix well again.

Serves 8 to 10

A SNIPPET FROM ONE SUMMER DAY

That day at the produce auction, Mrs. Bo and I bought large quantities of eggplant and many other items. From that one economical purchase, we were able to create several meals for our families. A produce auction is one of my favorite places to go in the summer. It meets many needs of my heart. It's so rewarding to find good, inexpensive food as I spend a day away from the routine of washing dishes and breaking up squabbles my children land in.

At one auction, I bought four crape myrtle trees, and my husband and I planted them along our driveway as a living memorial to our little baby, whom I had miscarried several years prior. Those trees bloom for six to eight weeks—right around the time he or she would have been born into our world. I live with a longing to meet that life we never got to hold. The trees remind me that we *will* meet this sweet soul when we cross the Jordan and enter into our heavenly reward. Isn't it wonderful how close heaven has come to me through those living crape myrtles and some beautiful and color-rich purple eggplants— both from an Amish produce auction? God is so amazing!

FRESH PINEAPPLE SALSA

4 large or 6 to 8 medium tomatoes, chopped

1 green pepper, diced

1 medium onion, diced

3 T. fresh cilantro, minced

Juice of 1 lemon or lime

1 tsp. or 2 garlic cloves, minced

1 tsp. salt (can add ½ tsp. more, but only after tasting, please)

½ tsp. black pepper

1 T. olive oil

2 tsp. vinegar

1 tsp. chili powder

1 tsp. cumin

¼ to ½ tsp. red pepper flakes (optional)

1 jalapeño, minced (optional)

1 to 1½ cups fresh pineapple or canned crushed pineapple, drained

1 to 2 tsp. sugar (optional)

The easiest way to make this salsa is to chop your tomatoes in the food processor and then place them in a strainer and allow the juice to drain for 5 minutes. After the tomatoes are chopped, chop the green pepper, onion, cilantro, and jalapeño in a food processer.

Place the chopped vegetables in a mixing bowl. Squeeze lemon or lime juice over the top. Add the garlic, salt, pepper, olive oil, vinegar, chili powder, cumin, and red pepper flakes. Stir until everything is mixed well. Then chop the fresh pineapple if you are using that. Mix the pineapple and optional sugar into the tomato mixture.

If the mixture seems too watery, drain off some of the liquid. (Note: Some tomatoes, such as Roma and Amish Paste, are meatier and have less liquid than other varieties.)

Yields 6 cups

HOMESTYLE HINT

You can easily use this same base recipe to make a black bean or corn salsa. Also, instead of pineapple, you can substitute peaches or fresh mango.

GRILLED EGGPLANT

My Italian friend, Mrs. Bo, taught me how to love eggplant. Bo has a large family, and she cooks very creatively for them. One day, she and I were driving to an Amish produce auction in Maryland. We were sharing food stories and talking candidly about life's challenges. Bo, who operates a flower farm on her homestead, has raised a lot of children. Because I homeschool my children, she is a world of wisdom to me. We love to share tips on how to feed our families good, wholesome, organic foods—and do it on the cheap. I am so blessed to do life with wise women around me!

> 3 to 4 garlic cloves
>
> 1 tsp. dried basil or 2 tsp. fresh basil, minced
>
> ½ cup olive oil
>
> 2 eggplants, each sliced into 6 pieces
>
> 1 cup pasta sauce
>
> 12 slices provolone cheese

Preheat the oven to 450°. With a fork, combine the garlic and basil. Stir in the olive oil. Drizzle this mixture over the eggplant. (If you still have oil left, turn over the eggplant slices and drizzle the other side.) Heat your grill to medium-high. Grill eggplants for 3 minutes per side and remove from heat.

Place the eggplant slices on a baking sheet and top with a tablespoon of pasta sauce and a piece of provolone cheese. Bake for 5 to 6 minutes or until the cheese is bubbly. (I don't like to over bake these, so I closely monitor the process.)

Serves 10 to 12

HOMESTYLE HINT

Rotisserie or grilled chicken breasts pair well with this side dish.

You can also create a meal for later by placing the eggplant slices on a parchment-lined baking sheet. Top with the pasta sauce and cheese and freeze for 12 to 24 hours. Once frozen, move the slices to a freezer bag for easier storage.

MARINADE FOR BBQ CHICKEN

- 1½ cups (3 sticks) butter, melted (or you can use half olive oil and half butter)
- ¾ cup Worcestershire sauce
- ¼ cup soy sauce or Bragg Liquid Aminos
- ½ cup vinegar
- 2 tsp. dry mustard powder
- 2 tsp. salt
- 1 tsp. black pepper
- 1 tsp. garlic powder

Combine all the ingredients into a resealable bag. Place chicken pieces in the bag and marinate for 12 to 24 hours. If you use boneless pieces, reduce the marinating time to 3 to 4 hours so the flavor won't be too intense. Grill to your liking.

Yields enough marinade for 3 to 5 pounds of bone-in chicken pieces

PESTO

 We sell bundles of basil at the little market where we also sell our blackberries and blueberries. I love to prepare fresh pesto in my blender.

By the way, pesto doesn't keep long in the refrigerator, but it freezes well. So when a long winter day has set in, you can pull out your frozen "summer abundance" and prepare a great pesto over spaghetti squash or pasta.

> 2 cups fresh basil, washed and dried between paper towels
>
> 3 garlic cloves
>
> ⅓ cup walnuts
>
> ½ to ¾ tsp. salt
>
> ¼ tsp. black pepper
>
> ⅔ cup olive oil
>
> ½ cup Parmesan cheese

Place the basil, garlic, walnuts, salt, and pepper in a blender. Blend for a minute or two, and then slowly add the olive oil. Put in a container and mix in the Parmesan cheese. Place in the refrigerator or divide into two containers, one for the refrigerator and the other for the freezer.

Yields 1½ cups of pesto

RED RASPBERRY POPPY SEED DRESSING

⅓ cup apple cider vinegar

½ cup raw sugar

¼ cup water

2 T. onion, minced

1 tsp. sea salt

1 tsp. ground mustard

1 cup olive oil

1 cup frozen red raspberries, thawed

1 tsp. poppy seeds

Pour all of the ingredients (except poppy seeds) into a blender. Blend thoroughly. Stir in the poppy seeds. Serve with a salad of your choice. (Please note that this dressing does not have a long refrigerator life. It needs to be used in 7 to 10 days.)

Yields 2 ½ cups

HOMESTYLE HINT

If you like a sweeter dressing, add more sugar to taste.

SUMMER APPLE SALAD

I recommend using several kinds of apples here for a variety of colors and flavors. A combination of tart and sweet tastes great in this salad. Think Granny Smith plus Gala.

5 to 6 cups apples, cored and diced (about 5 to 7 apples)

1 cup red grapes, washed

2 cups small marshmallows

1 cup celery (optional)

2 cups whipping cream

½ cup powdered sugar

¼ cup mayonnaise

½ cup sour cream

¼ cup sugar

2 T. vinegar

¼ tsp. salt

Wash and dice the apples. Place the apples in a large mixing bowl and then add the grapes, marshmallows, and celery, if using.

Beat the whipping cream until soft peaks start to form. Add the powdered sugar and beat until stiff peaks form.

In a separate bowl, combine the mayonnaise, sour cream, sugar, vinegar, and salt. Add to the apple mixture and stir. Add the whipping cream and stir just until combined. Serve or refrigerate until ready to use.

Serves 12

HOMESTYLE HINT

You can shortcut this recipe by purchasing prepared coleslaw dressing. Use 1¼ cups of this dressing in place of the mayo, sour cream, sugar, vinegar, and salt.

STUFFED ZUCCHINI

Are you unsure of what to do with all the zucchinis growing in your garden? Here's a pretty good way of using some of them.

2 medium zucchinis

½ lb. ground sausage

¼ cup onion, chopped

1 clove garlic, minced

⅔ cup seasoned bread crumbs

½ cup milk

⅛ tsp. dill weed

1 cup spaghetti sauce

½ cup white cheddar cheese, shredded

Preheat the oven to 350°. Cut the zucchinis in half lengthwise and scoop out the pulp, leaving one-quarter-inch shells. Chop up the pulp and set aside.

In a skillet, brown the sausage, onion, and garlic; drain. Add the pulp, bread crumbs, milk, dill weed, and spaghetti sauce. Mix well and then spoon into the zucchini boats. Top with the cheese. Cover and bake for 35 minutes or until the zucchini shells are tender.

Serves 4 to 6

TUNA SALAD FOR ONE

This is my busy-mom lunch. If I have cucumbers and tomatoes growing in my garden, it makes me happy to harvest them for this recipe. And tuna is something I always keep on hand. This is a great low-carb lunch!

½ cup cucumber, diced

1 medium tomato, diced

1½ tsp. onion, minced

1 (5 oz.) can tuna, rinsed and drained

2 T. Italian dressing

1 tsp. fresh basil, minced (optional)

Salt and pepper to taste

Dice the cucumber and tomato and mince the onion. Combine with the tuna, dressing, basil, salt, and pepper.

Serves 1

ZUCCHINI SAUTÉ

2 to 3 zucchini (or a mix of zucchini and another summer squash,
   4 cups total)

1 medium onion

1 to 2 T. butter

2 T. Italian dressing

Salt and pepper to taste

¼ cup tomatoes, diced

2 T. shredded Parmesan cheese

1 tsp. fresh basil, minced (or ½ tsp. dried)

Wash and slice the zucchini. Mince or thinly slice the onion.
Melt butter in a kettle on medium-high heat. Add the onion
and stir fry for 3 to 4 minutes. Add the zucchini and sauté
for 5 to 6 minutes. If the mixture cooks too dry, add a bit
more butter. Turn off heat and add the Italian dressing, salt,
and pepper. Stir and then garnish with tomatoes, shredded
Parmesan, and basil. Serve immediately.

Serves 4 to 6

BLACKBERRY GOODNESS

We grow blackberries in our garden, and I can hardly wait until I have picked a quart of them so that I can make this wonderful dish. Sometimes, getting a quart or two can be a challenge because of the weather. Other times, it's because when I am out working in my garden and the sun has warmed these black jewels, it's just plain hard to avoid snacking on them. If you've not had the privilege of eating a sun-warmed berry, please come to my garden. I would love to share the experience with you. It's pure goodness.

½ cup water

1½ T. cornstarch

½ cup sugar

1½ qt. blackberries

1 cup flour

1½ tsp. baking powder

½ tsp. salt

¼ cup butter

¼ cup milk

1 egg, beaten

Preheat the oven to 400°. Blend the water, cornstarch, and sugar. Pour over the washed berries in a medium saucepan and bring to a boil. Boil 15 minutes or until the mixture thickens. Pour into an 8 x 8-inch baking dish.

Next, combine the flour, baking powder, and salt. Cut in butter, until the mixture resembles peas.

In a separate bowl, combine the milk and egg. Add to the flour mixture, stirring just until moist.

Spoon the dough on top of the berries

Bake for 20 minutes or until the top is golden brown.

Serves 6 to 8

CHOCOLATE CHIP COOKIES

We homeschool our children, which requires much of my energy—sometimes more energy than I think I have to give. But summer allows me time to breathe, to stop pushing myself so hard, and to catch up on projects that have been shoved into the closet. I look forward to this precious season, which never seems long enough.

Not long ago, on one of the first days of summer vacation, my strong and brave eight-year-old came to me, bored and wanting me to find something for him to do. I made a mental note to have a talk with God about patience with this young man, who is so full of questions and comments.

The next morning, I found myself pouring out my heart to God. "How can I channel the endless and restless energy of my firstborn?" The Lord showed up, and it was as if I heard Him say, "Teach him how to make chocolate chip cookies."

My response: "Are You sure, Lord? He's only eight years old."

Thirty minutes later, I related this story to my son. I told him I would teach him how to bake cookies, but it would be later, in the afternoon. Two hours later (when it was still morning), he said, "Mom, can you teach me now?"

I had to remind him about the time. Finally, at about three o'clock, I showed him the recipe, step by step, and we baked some cookies. They were delicious. The venture was a success, but I thought he would need several more lessons before he became proficient.

The next morning, a Saturday, my son greeted me with, "Hey, Mom, can I bake chocolate chip cookies today?"

"Uh, sure, son. But I won't be around because I have errands to run. Are you sure you're ready?"

"Ready!" he said. The rest is history.

I came home that afternoon to perfectly baked cookies. They were better than the ones we baked together the previous day.

He's been making fantastic cookies ever since. He bakes cookies for my small group, for Sunday school classes, and for the neighbors as a treat. And the list goes on.

I am not sure why I was so surprised at such a quick and specific answer to my summertime prayer. After all, our God is such a personal God. So when I shared my frustration over my son's boundless energy, He showed me how to channel that young energy for His glory.

What irritates or frustrates you today? Perhaps there is a very personal solution to your problem. Perhaps it's just a prayer away, and all you need to do is ask. In our human frailty, we sometimes overlook the most obvious lifeline. Trust me. God is truly a Father who loves to give us good gifts.

Here is that answer-to-prayer recipe.

> 1 cup (2 sticks) butter, room temperature
>
> ¾ cup brown sugar
>
> 2 eggs
>
> ½ tsp. salt
>
> 1 tsp. vanilla
>
> 1 (3.4 oz.) box instant vanilla pudding
>
> 2¼ cups flour
>
> 1 tsp. baking soda
>
> 1 cup semisweet chocolate chips

Preheat the oven to 350°. Cream the butter and brown sugar together, and then mix in the eggs. Next, stir in the salt, vanilla, instant pudding, flour, and baking soda. Add the chocolate chips and stir again. Form the dough into balls and bake for 8 to 9 minutes on a baking stone.

Yields about 3 dozen

CHOCOLATE-COVERED STRAWBERRIES WITH WHITE CHOCOLATE DRIZZLE

 These sweet treats are an all-time crowd pleaser. They are very simple to make, but they feel special.

1 qt. strawberries, rinsed and dried, with stems intact

1 (12 oz.) pkg. milk chocolate wafers

2 T. shortening

½ cup white chocolate wafers, for drizzle

After the berries have dried, combine the milk chocolate wafers and shortening in the top of a double boiler, adding a half cup of water to the boiler's bottom section. Place on a burner set to medium. Heat and stir until chocolate is completely melted and smooth. Do not overheat.

Dip the strawberries in chocolate, leaving the tops of the berries and the stems exposed.

Place the strawberries on waxed paper or parchment. Wait until the chocolate has hardened and then melt the white chocolate wafers in the double boiler. Using a skewer, drizzle the white chocolate over the strawberries.

Yield varies

EASY-AS-PIE CUSTARD PIE

This is my sister's recipe, and boy, is it delicious! Baking a custard pie always seemed to be difficult until she gave me this recipe.

2 cups milk

4 eggs, well beaten

1 cup sugar

1 tsp. vanilla

1 unbaked pie shell

Preheat the oven to 450°. Bring the milk to a rolling boil and then remove the pan from heat. Beat the eggs until well-beaten and add the sugar and vanilla. Add the milk to the egg mixture, beating slightly. Pour the custard into the unbaked pie shell and bake for 15 minutes.

Serves 8 to 12

FRESH STRAWBERRY OR PEACH PIE

We served a similar version of this dessert at the Farmer's Wife, a small bakery, deli, and bulk food store my husband and I owned until our first two kids came along. There were days we could not peel enough peaches to keep our peach pie in stock. It was so satisfying to serve something people truly enjoyed. This was one of my favorite items—not because of the amount of work that went into it, but because I knew folks would not be disappointed when they sank their teeth into this deliciousness!

PIE GLAZE

1 cup sugar

½ cup Clear Jel (You can purchase this thickening agent at a bulk-food store or on Amazon.com.)

Pinch of salt

2 cups lemon-lime soda

2 cups water

1½ tsp. lemon juice

3 oz. peach or strawberry gelatin (depending on your choice of fruit)

In a saucepan, stir together the sugar, Clear Jel, and salt. Add the lemon-lime soda, water, and lemon juice. Cook over high heat for 3 minutes, stirring constantly. Reduce the temperature to medium-high and continue to stir constantly so that the Clear Jel doesn't get lumpy. This mixture should thicken in about 5 minutes and lose its watery consistency.

Remove from heat and stir in the gelatin. Place a piece of plastic wrap on top of the hot glaze so that it doesn't form a crust. Refrigerate 3 to 4 hours.

You should have enough glaze (4 cups) to fill two 9-inch, extra-deep pie crusts. Any extra glaze can be stored in the refrigerator, in an airtight container, for up to 2 weeks. Place plastic wrap over your container before putting the lid on it.

PIE

8 medium-large peaches or 1½ lbs. fresh strawberries

2 cups cooled glaze (recipe above)

1 baked pie shell

1 cup whipping cream

¼ tsp. powdered sugar

1 tsp. vanilla

Peel and dice peaches (or slice strawberries). Mix into glaze. Place this mixture into pie shell(s). Beat the whipping cream until soft peaks form. Add powdered sugar and vanilla and beat until blended and whipping cream holds its shape. Top the fruit mixture with the whipped cream and enjoy.

Serves 6 to 8

HOMESTYLE HINT

Instead of using the glaze for a pie, you can use it to top an angel food cake. Make a cream cheese filling, if you desire, and serve slices of cake with several tablespoons of the filling and fresh fruit mixed together.

FRUIT PIZZA

FIRST LAYER

4 eggs, beaten until light

1¼ cups sugar

1 tsp. vanilla

1 cup hot water

2 cups flour

2 tsp. baking powder

Pinch of salt

Preheat the oven to 350°. Mix the eggs, sugar, vanilla, and water until combined. Then add the dry ingredients and mix well. Pour the batter into a jelly roll-sized pan and bake for 15 minutes. Let cool.

SECOND LAYER

12 oz. cream cheese, softened

1 cup powdered sugar

1 cup whipping cream, whipped

Beat the cream cheese with the powdered sugar and then fold in the whipped cream. Spread on the baked layer.

THIRD LAYER

4 cups fresh fruit, sliced

Arrange the fruit slices on top of your pizza, arranged to your liking.

FOURTH LAYER

¾ cup sugar

1 cup water or fruit juice

2 T. Clear Jel

2 T. peach Jell-O

In a small saucepan, dissolve the sugar into the water or juice on medium-high heat. Dissolve the Clear Jel with a little water and then add it to the saucepan. Cook the liquid until thickened.

Remove from the heat and add the Jell-O. Let the glaze cool slightly, and then pour over the fruit slices.

Serves 12

ITALIAN CREAM SODA

How about a coffee-shop drink right in your home? My Aunt Rose introduced our family to this delicious beverage when she visited us for Thanksgiving a few years ago. Aunt Rose is actually younger than I am and is more like a sister. She breathed so much life into our lives that visit, and we really needed it, as our son Will was sick during the holiday season. We sampled these sodas over Thanksgiving weekend, and we've been hooked ever since. She even went out and purchased more of the ingredients while visiting so we could enjoy them long after her visit. I keep everything on hand so that we are always ready for a random celebration! Our favorite is when Merv, my husband, declares a family date on the deck with a special drink. This is always our first choice!

> Ice
> 6 to 8 oz. sparkling water
> ¼ cup fruit-flavored coffeehouse syrup
> 2 T. half-and-half

Fill a pretty glass with ice. Add sparkling water, flavored syrup, and half-and-half. Add a straw, stir, and enjoy to the last drop!

Serves 1

A KITCHEN PSALM

Psalm 15:1-2 says, "Lord, who may dwell in your sacred tent? Who may live on your holy mountain? The one whose walk is blameless, who does what is righteous, who speaks the truth from their heart." When I am at work in the kitchen, this Scripture is often on my heart. I find myself praying, "I will praise You with my whole, messy soul!" Yes, it is messy on some days, but I am so grateful I am still able to dwell in His sanctuary, in the shelter of His peace. What a gift!

LEMON RASPBERRY MUFFINS

2 eggs, beaten

½ cup milk

½ cup lemon yogurt

4 T. butter, melted

1 tsp. vanilla

2 cups flour

1 T. baking powder

⅔ cup sugar

2 tsp. lemon zest, divided

1 tsp. salt

2 cups raspberries

2 T. lemon juice

½ cup powdered sugar

Preheat the oven to 350°. Combine the eggs, milk, yogurt, butter, and vanilla in a medium-sized bowl. Set aside.

In a separate bowl, stir together the flour, baking powder, sugar, 1 teaspoon lemon zest, and salt. Stir the egg mixture into the flour mixture and then gently fold in the raspberries.

Drop the batter into greased muffin tins with an ice cream scoop. Bake for 18 to 20 minutes.

In a small bowl, combine the lemon juice, powdered sugar, and the remaining teaspoon of lemon zest. Brush this lemon glaze over the muffins once they have cooled to just warm.

Yields 12 muffins

LEMON RASPBERRY NO-BAKE CHEESECAKE

This is one summery and refreshing dessert! Imagine eating this outside in your oasis on a lazy summer day. What is it about lemon and raspberry that says "summer," plain and simple?

CRUST

> 18 graham crackers, crushed
>
> 6 T. sugar
>
> ¾ cup (1½ sticks) butter, melted

Combine the ingredients and then press the mixture into a 9 x 13-inch baking pan to form a crust.

CHEESECAKE FILLING

> 3 (8 oz.) pkgs. cream cheese
>
> 1½ cups powdered sugar
>
> 2 cups heavy whipping cream
>
> ¾ cup berry-lemonade mix (I like Country Time brand)

Beat the cream cheese and powdered sugar together. Add the whipping cream and beat until well mixed. Add lemonade mix and blend well.

Spread the cream cheese mixture over graham cracker crust and chill until firm.

Cut into squares and garnish with lemon slices and fresh red raspberries.

Serves 15

PEACH HALF-MOON PIES

This is another one of my favorites to serve at a ladies' luncheon. These pies are so fun to eat and so summery. And they're kid friendly!

1 T. butter

4 tsp. cornstarch

⅓ cup sugar (adjust the amount of sugar depending on the sweetness or tartness of your peaches)

5 to 6 peaches, peeled, pitted, and sliced

1¼ tsp. ground cinnamon

¼ tsp. salt

1 T. lemon juice

4 (9-inch) pie crusts

1 egg, beaten

Melt the butter in a skillet. Combine cornstarch with sugar and add to skillet. Stir in peaches, cinnamon, and salt. Cook until the mixture boils and thickens, about 20 to 25 minutes. Be sure to stir frequently. Remove from heat and stir in lemon juice. Cool completely for easier handling.

Cut the pie crusts into quarters. Spoon 2 tablespoons of peach filling into the center of each quarter, leaving a half-inch dough border. Fold crust in half over the filling, pressing the edges with a fork to seal. Place the pies on two ungreased baking sheets. Brush tops of the pies with the beaten egg. Cut a one-inch slit in the top of each pie to let steam escape. Bake at 425° for 18 to 20 minutes. Remove to wire racks for cooling.

Makes 16 pies

RED RASPBERRY BARS WITH CRUMB TOPPING

These fruit bars are tasty and are delicious when served with ice cream. The neat thing about this recipe is that if you don't have raspberries, perhaps you have blackberries or blueberries. They will work fine. Just change up the berries. It's all good!

1½ cups (3 sticks) butter, divided	3 T. cornstarch
⅔ cup powdered sugar	2 T. water
1 tsp. vanilla	1 cup quick oats, uncooked
3 cups flour, divided	⅓ cup brown sugar
3 pints berries	½ tsp. cinnamon
½ cup sugar	Powdered sugar for dusting

Preheat the oven to 375°. Beat 1 cup of the butter (2 sticks), powdered sugar, and vanilla with a mixer until light and fluffy. Beat in 2½ cups flour on very low speed, just until combined. Press the dough into a greased jelly roll pan. Bake for 15 minutes and let cool.

Combine the berries, sugar, cornstarch, and water in a saucepan. Bring to boiling, stirring frequently. Boil for 1 minute and then remove from heat.

Reduce the heat in the oven to 350°. To make the crumb topping, mix the remaining flour, quick oats, brown sugar, and cinnamon in a medium bowl. Cut in the remaining 1 stick of butter (mixture will be crumbly). Pour the berry mixture over the dough and top with the crumb mixture. Bake for 40 minutes.

When serving these bars, cut them into squares and dust with powdered sugar.

Yield approximately 20 bars

RED RASPBERRY TORTE

The tartness of red raspberries pairs so well with a cream filling. My mother grows heirloom red raspberries on her farm—carrying on a tradition begun more than one hundred years ago when my great-great-grandfather homesteaded the farm. There really is nothing as sweet as an heirloom red raspberry. They are much smaller than the cultivated red raspberries (which we all still love), and they are oh-so-sweet. One of my nieces, Brooklyn, once told my mother, "Grandma, you make the best raspberries!"

Yes, Grandma, you do.

CRUST

1¼ cups flour

2 T. sugar

1 cup walnuts, chopped

¾ cup (1½ sticks) butter, melted

Preheat the oven to 325°. In a bowl, combine the flour, sugar, walnuts, and butter. Press into an 8 x 11-inch oven-safe baking dish and bake for 15 to 18 minutes. Cool for 1 hour, or quick-cool in your refrigerator for about 15 minutes.

CREAM FILLING

2 cups whipping cream

2 (8 oz.) pkgs. cream cheese, room temperature

1¾ cups powdered sugar

2 tsp. vanilla extract

¼ tsp. salt

In a large mixing bowl, beat the whipping cream until stiff peaks start to form. Set aside.

In another bowl, beat the cream cheese until smooth, and then add the powdered sugar, vanilla, and salt. Beat well, stopping once to stir the sides of the bowl so that you don't have a lumpy mixture. Once the cream cheese mixture is smooth, add the whipping cream just until combined. Pour this mixture over the cooled crust and refrigerate.

TOPPING

    1 (6 oz.) pkg. raspberry gelatin

    ½ cup sugar

    1 cup boiling water

    24 oz. frozen red raspberries, thawed and partially drained

Dissolve the gelatin and sugar in the boiling water and let sit 30 minutes. Once that has thickened, add the raspberries and then pour the topping over the pie filling. Garnish with mint leaves.

Serves 9

REFRESHING SLUSH ICE CUBES

This is another one of those wonderful summer drinks that truly hits the spot on hot days when you need refreshment after working in the fields or in the garden. These cubes are also great for summer cookouts. I was introduced to these by my friend Ruth Ann. I hope you will enjoy them as much as I have.

4 cups water

1 cup sugar

1 (12 oz.) can frozen orange juice concentrate

½ cup lemon juice

1 (46 oz.) can pineapple juice

Heat water and sugar. Adding remaining ingredients and stir well. Pour into ice cube trays and freeze. To serve, fill a glass with cubes and add lemon-lime soda or ginger ale.

Makes 40 to 50 cubes

HOMESTYLE HINT

These cubes can be removed from trays and stored in a plastic container in the freezer for up to 6 months.

ZUCCHINI BREAD

3 eggs

2 cups sugar

1 cup vegetable oil

3 tsp. vanilla

2 tsp. baking soda

1 tsp. baking powder

2½ cups flour

2 cups zucchini, grated

Beat the eggs and then add the sugar and oil and beat for an additional 5 minutes (to make your bread lighter). Add the rest of ingredients until well mixed. Pour into greased loaf pans and bake at 350° for 1 hour.

Makes 3 medium-sized loaves and freezes well

FALL

MAIN DISHES
Baked Potato Soup
Baked Salmon
Cheesy Noodle and Broccoli Soup
Creamy Autumn Soup
Oodles of Noodles
Pumpkin Cinnamon Baked Oatmeal
Roasted Rosemary Turkey
Sausage Cheese Soup
Scalloped Potatoes
Spaghetti Squash Supreme
Sweet Potato Casserole
Turkey Sausage, Sweet Potato, and Apple Bake
White Chicken Chili
Yumesetti

SAUCES, SIDE DISHES, AND SALADS
Bacon Brussels Sprouts
Bountiful Harvest Salad
Butterscotch Apple Salad
Cinnamon Red Hots Applesauce
Cooked Apples
Cranberry Waldorf Salad
Easy-Bake Butternut or Acorn Squash
Roasted Potatoes
Sausage Gravy
Slow-Cooker Apple Butter
Sweet Potato Soufflé

Dawn's recipes are marked with a 🌿, and Carol's with a 🌾.

SNACKS AND DESSERTS

Apple Crescents

Apple Crisp

Butterscotch Cream Pie

Caramel Corn

Date Pudding

Fresh Apple Bars with Cinnamon Cream Cheese Frosting

Good Morning Muffins

Hot Apple Cider

Pumpkin Bars with Cream Cheese Icing

Pumpkin Cookies with Maple Cream Cheese Frosting

Pumpkin Dip

Pumpkin Granola Balls

Pumpkin Muffins

Dawn's recipes are marked with a , and Carol's with a .

Fall is a time of harvest, a gathering for our families, and it can also be a time of gathering into our souls. A time to stop and behold the beauty in the colors, the crunch in the crisp leaves beneath our feet. It also brings a borderline-compulsive obsession for me to purge. I find myself wanting to clean every crowded corner and to organize all of our books. Maybe it's so I can truly breathe when winter comes—*if* the fall list gets done. I recognize we all have a favorite season we gravitate to, but I think if we can approach our hearts in the same way we approach the seasons, there is always space to learn and grow.

BAKED POTATO SOUP

This soup is definitely a comfort food. I love putting it in my slow cooker because I enjoy the wonderful smells as I anticipate eating it for dinner.

4 large potatoes

12 slices bacon

⅔ cup butter

⅔ cup flour

6 cups whole milk

¾ tsp. salt

½ tsp. pepper

4 green onions, chopped and divided

2 cups cheddar cheese, shredded

4 slices American cheese

1 cup sour cream

Wash the potatoes in cold water and then prick them with a fork or knife. Place them directly on the oven's baking rack or on a baking sheet and bake them at 350° for 1 hour. When the potatoes are cool enough to handle, cut them in half and scoop out the pulp; set aside.

Fry the bacon until crisp and then cool and crumble.

Melt the butter in a large kettle and then sprinkle on the flour. Gradually stir in the milk. Continue to stir until the white sauce is smooth, thickened, and bubbly. Add the potato pulp, salt, pepper, bacon, cheese, and three-fourths of the green onions. Cook until heated. Transfer to a slow cooker, cover, and set on low for 4 hours.

Just before serving, stir in the sour cream and top with the remaining green onions.

Serves 6 to 8

BAKED SALMON

This is probably one of my quickest go-to meals. I almost always have salmon fillets and green beans in our freezer, and rice in the cupboard. I can place rice in my rice cooker, and it can do its thing while I am wrapping up school lessons or other projects.

1 lb. salmon fillet (or as many smaller fillets as needed)

Paprika, garlic powder, salt, and pepper to taste

2 to 3 T. butter

Preheat the oven to 400°. Place the salmon in a baking dish or baking pan lined with parchment paper. Sprinkle with the above seasonings. Slice thin pats of butter over the salmon and bake for 8 or 11 minutes. (You can make a delicious variation of this dish by adding 2 tablespoons of honey to your spice mixture. And if you close up the parchment paper and seal in the salmon well, the edges won't be as crispy.)

Serves 4

HOMESTYLE HINT

Salmon can be tricky to bake because fillets tend to differ in thickness. Here's a good rule of thumb: Bake salmon (at 400 degrees) for 5 minutes per half-inch of thickness. This will help you avoid overbaking the salmon and drying it out.

CHEESY NOODLE AND BROCCOLI SOUP

2 cups fresh broccoli

3 T. butter

2 cloves garlic

4 cups water

2 cups chicken broth

8 oz. noodles

2 cups whole milk

1 lb. American cheese

1 tsp. salt

Freshly ground pepper to taste

Soy sauce to taste

Steam the broccoli until tender, chop, and set aside.

In a soup pot, melt the butter until browned and add the garlic. Cook about 2 minutes and then add the water and chicken broth and bring the liquid to a boil. Add the noodles. When noodles are soft (about 8 to 10 minutes), add the broccoli, milk, and cheese.

Heat until hot, but do not allow the soup to boil. Add the salt and a couple of turns of freshly ground pepper and a dash or two or maybe three of soy sauce.

Serves 10 to 12

CREAMY AUTUMN SOUP

Our pastor's wife brought us some autumn soup one Saturday night when our little son Will Franklin was very sick with whooping cough. Our family was in survival mode during this season in our lives. We were walking *hard*! So Mrs. Susie's soup did more than feed our tummies. It fed our souls. I firmly believe we can love people well by reaching out with food during their hard times. It doesn't have to be anything elaborate. It can be a simple rotisserie chicken purchased at the grocery store. On that Saturday, the soup's yumminess let me know that God was present, right in the middle of our hard times. He saw our specific need for that day.

If you're working in your kitchen and you feel an urging in your soul to reach out to someone, don't ignore that. In our story, Mrs. Susie had simply made too much soup for her and her husband, Pastor Bob. Then she thought of us. Like Mrs. Susie, you can really make a difference as an agent of Jesus. You can be the difference between a soul in utter despair and a soul feeling cared for and loved.

By the way, this is a creamy and rich soup. Your kids won't even notice the healthy amount of vegetables hidden in it. Score!

3½ to 4 lbs. butternut squash chunks
½ cup water
2½ cups onion, chopped (Yes, this much!)
2 T. butter
8 cups chicken broth
2 cups cooked brown rice
24 oz. turkey kielbasa sausage, sliced thin
1 (15 oz.) can whole kernel corn
1 (15 oz.) can cream style corn
1 tsp. salt
½ tsp. black pepper
¼ tsp. red pepper flakes (optional)
1 cup half-and-half

Cook the squash and water on very low heat, until the squash is quite soft, about 20 to 30 minutes. Allow to cool a bit, and then puree it in a food processor or blender until it's smooth.

In a stock pot, sauté the butter and onion for 4 to 5 minutes. Add the chicken broth and cook until boiling. Add the pureed squash, rice, kielbasa, corn, salt, and pepper. Heat until desired temperature is reached, but do not bring to a boil. Remove from heat and add half-and-half.

Serves 10 to 12

OODLES OF NOODLES

If you are cooking for a crowd of people—even a crowd of 100—this is an easy recipe. And it's tasty too. Of course, it can be adjusted for smaller crowds.

1 cup (2 sticks) butter

4 qt. chicken broth

6 qt. water

8 oz. chicken soup base

2 (28 oz.) cans cream of chicken soup

5 lbs. noodles (your choice—we prefer Inn Maid Egg Noodles)

Salt and pepper to taste

In a 20-quart stock pot, melt butter until golden brown. Add the chicken broth, water, and soup base. Bring to a boil. Stir in cream of chicken soup. Bring to *almost* boiling and then add the noodles and salt and pepper. Stir and bring to a full boil again. Turn off heat and cover with a lid. Do not remove lid until ready to serve. Allow to set for 1 hour before serving.

These noodles are delicious. Yes, the preparation time seems daunting, but while your noodles are setting, you can tackle other tasks.

This recipe easily serves 50 people

PUMPKIN CINNAMON BAKED OATMEAL

¼ cup butter or coconut oil, melted

3 eggs

1 cup Sucanat or brown sugar

½ cup plain Greek yogurt

1 cup pumpkin puree

1 cup milk or 1¼ cups almond milk

3 cups old-fashioned oatmeal

1½ tsp. baking powder

1 tsp. sea salt

2 tsp. ground cinnamon

Preheat the oven to 350°. Mix the butter or oil, eggs, Sucanat or brown sugar, yogurt, pumpkin puree, and milk. Add the oatmeal, baking powder, salt, and cinnamon. Stir just until combined.

Pour into an 8 x 11-inch baking dish and bake for 30 to 35 minutes. Bake for 25 to 30 minutes if using a 9 x 13-inch pan. Serve with warm milk.

Serves 6 to 8

ROASTED ROSEMARY TURKEY

Confession: Turkey is one of my least favorite meats. I know it's a leaner choice than other meats, but there is something about it that I just don't love. But, for the one time of year when I cook a whole bird, this is the recipe I like to use.

According to my friends Shawn and Katrina, who run a nursing home and cook five turkeys every Thanksgiving, the key to a moist bird is to prepare the turkey three or four days in advance. Carve the bird and return it to its pan juices. As it sits in the liquid, it stays moist. Before serving time, reheat it just until hot. It truly does make for a more delicate white meat.

1 (15 lb.) turkey

2 onions, quartered

4 garlic cloves

2 apples, quartered

½ cup (1 stick) butter

3 T. rosemary, dried

8 garlic cloves, minced

2 T. seasoning salt

1 tsp. black pepper

1 tsp. paprika

In a large roasting pan, place the turkey breast-side down. Stuff the bird's cavity with the onions, garlic, and apples. Liberally salt the outside.

In a small saucepan, melt the butter. Remove from heat and add the rosemary, garlic, seasoning salt, black pepper, and paprika. Pour this mixture over top of the bird. Rinse the butter pan with 2 cups warm water, and pour this water into your roasting pan, to the side of the bird, rather than on it, so you don't rinse off your seasonings. Cover tightly and roast the turkey according to the package directions.

Remove from the oven. When the turkey has cooled enough, place it back in the juices. Refrigerate the turkey until the day you want to serve it. Reheat the bird at 350° for 45 minutes to an hour, or until heated throughout.

Serves about 15 people

HOMESTYLE HINT

When baking a whole turkey, it's best to figure approximately one pound per person.

SAUSAGE CHEESE SOUP

2 cups potatoes, diced

1 lb. bulk sausage

2 cloves fresh garlic, minced

4 cups whole milk

1 tsp. chives

1 tsp. celery salt

1 tsp. parsley flakes

Salt and pepper to taste

2 cups cheddar cheese, shredded

Boil the potatoes in 2 cups of water until soft; set aside (do not drain the potatoes). In a skillet, fry the sausage and the garlic. When done, add the sausage to the potatoes. Then add the milk and seasonings. Heat until good and hot but not boiling.

Remove from heat and stir in cheese, allowing it to melt before serving.

Serves 6

SCALLOPED POTATOES

10 lbs. potatoes, sliced

2 qt. milk

1½ cups flour

2 T. salt

½ tsp. pepper

1¼ cup butter

1 medium onion, chopped

2 tsp. Worcestershire sauce

1 lb. Velveeta cheese

5 lbs. ham, cubed

Cook the potatoes in salted water, cool, and shred.

In a large saucepan over medium-high heat, make a sauce of the milk, flour, salt, pepper, butter, onion, Worcestershire sauce, and Velveeta cheese.

Add the potatoes and the ham to the sauce and mix well. Place in two 9 x 13-inch baking pans and bake at 350° for 1 hour.

Serves 25 to 30

SPAGHETTI SQUASH SUPREME

 This is a low-carb dish, and the kids will eat it. Score!

2 spaghetti squashes, approximately 6 to 8 cups total

2 lbs. ground sausage

2½ cups mozzarella cheese

8 oz. cream cheese, softened

1 cup whipping cream

1 tsp. salt

¼ tsp. pepper

3 garlic cloves, minced

2 T. parsley

Wash and halve the squashes. Place cut side down on a parchment-lined cookie sheet. Bake at 375° for 60 minutes. (Or use the slow-cooker method, described in Homestyle Hint for "Baked Spaghetti Squash" on page 65.)

Scoop out seeds. With a fork, remove the squash, which will resemble spaghetti noodles. Place them in a bowl. Add the sausage and mozzarella cheese.

In another bowl, lightly beat the cream cheese until smooth. Add the whipping cream, salt, pepper, garlic, and parsley. Add the cream cheese mixture to squash mixture. Stir just until slightly mixed, pour into a 9 x 13-inch baking dish, and bake at 350° for 60 minutes.

Serves 6 to 8

HOMESTYLE HINT

I like to cook my sausage in my slow cooker so I don't have to fry it over a hot stove. I often cook up to 6 pounds at a time this way and freeze some for later. It's so nice to have this step done ahead of time.

SWEET POTATO CASSEROLE

 This recipe is a Thanksgiving favorite, even among some of the grandchildren.

3 cups canned yams, drained

1 cup brown sugar, divided

½ tsp. salt

½ cup milk

⅓ cup flour

3 T. butter, softened

¾ cup pecans, chopped

Preheat the oven to 350°. In a bowl, combine the yams with half a cup of the brown sugar, salt, and milk. Put in a lightly greased 1½-quart casserole dish.

Next, mix together the remaining ½ cup brown sugar, flour, butter, and pecans. Spread over top of sweet potatoes and bake for 30 minutes.

Serves 6

TURKEY SAUSAGE, SWEET POTATO, AND APPLE BAKE

This is a simple one-dish meal. You can add or subtract ingredients to accommodate your family's preferences. This dish is especially fun for me because we've raised our own sweet potatoes over the past couple of years. It's so rewarding to store our own garden produce in the basement, where it's ready for a recipe like this.

1 small sweet potato per family member (I use four "big daddies" for our family of six. When you grow your own potatoes, they come in a variety of shapes and sizes.)

6 turkey sausage kielbasas

1 large apple or 2 small apples, sliced in big chunks

4 to 6 sprigs fresh thyme (optional) or ½ tsp. dried thyme

2 T. butter (more if you're not concerned about your carb/fat ratio)

Salt and pepper to taste

Peel and chunk the sweet potatoes. Add the sausage, sliced apples, thyme, butter, and salt and pepper. Cover tightly and bake at 375° for 1 hour. For a more golden bake, remove foil for the last 15 minutes of baking.

Serves 4 to 6

WHITE CHICKEN CHILI

 This is my favorite chili recipe. It's filled with flavor and lots of just plain goodness.

1 lb. skinless, boneless chicken breasts

2 T. oil

1 T. minced garlic

2 tsp. chili powder

4 T. butter

½ cup flour

4 cups chicken broth

1 (24 oz.) jar Great Northern Beans

Salt and pepper to taste

1 tsp. garlic salt

2 cups half-and-half

6 slices white American cheese

Cut the chicken breasts into cubes and cook them in the oil over medium-high heat. Set aside.

In a soup pot, sauté the garlic and chili powder in the butter. Sprinkle on flour and stir until bubbly, and then slowly add the chicken broth, cooking until thickened.

Stir in beans, chicken, salt and pepper, and garlic salt; bring to a boil. Turn down the heat to low and then add the half-and-half and cheese until thoroughly heated.

Serves 6 to 8

YUMESETTI

Here's something we made all of the time on the farm. This simple one-dish meal is sure to fill everyone up. You can either layer the hamburger and noodles or just mix everything together and top with cheese. You can make this dish more healthful by adding a layer of frozen peas or other vegetables.

2 lbs. hamburger

½ cup onion, diced

13.25 oz. angel hair pasta or 16 oz. egg noodles (we like Dreamfields pastas)

1 (29 oz.) can tomato sauce

12 oz. of your favorite mushroom soup

1 lb. white American cheese, ripped into small pieces

¼ cup water

½ tsp. salt

¼ tsp. black pepper

½ tsp. garlic powder

Preheat the oven to 350°. Fry the hamburger and onion together. While waiting for the hamburger to cook thoroughly, cook pasta al dente and drain. Combine all other ingredients and place in a 9 x 13-baking dish.

Cover with foil and bake for 30 minutes. Remove foil and bake uncovered for an additional 15 minutes.

Serves 10 to 12

HOMESTYLE HINT

You can easily double this recipe and freeze one casserole for a later date.

QUALITY TIME

We can tend to grow cynical about the concept of God being with us in our daily lives, but if our souls are open to "aha moments," we will realize how often God comes to us, in love, through one of His people. God is with us everywhere.

For this slice of time in my children's lives, I want their senses to be fully engaged. I want their mouths to taste the deliciousness all around them, their ears to hear beautiful music, their eyes to see beauty. I want their small hands to touch the beautiful things all around us. When I help my children to fully engage their senses, it opens pathways to their souls. Then they listen to my messages, whether it's a message about table manners or a story of God's faithfulness.

I've found I can best help open up my children's souls by spending special time with each one of them. On a semi-regular basis, I take each child to my bedroom for 45 minutes or so, time when they have my undivided attention. We light a candle and enjoy a cup of cocoa and cookies or a few pieces of chocolate. (I always keep a batch of cookie dough balls in my freezer ready to bake for times such as these.)

Their eyes sparkle just a bit more knowing they matter to me—that they have my full attention and don't have to share it with one of their siblings. I try to schedule these times once a month or every other month. I don't want it to become an obligation for me, but I realize this space in time is an eternal investment, and that my time with them, when they are like little sponges, is so short.

I want this to be the place where they share their struggles, their pain, and the things buried in their hearts. It's also an opportunity for me to address hard topics. But sometimes we will just play games or read a book they have been waiting patiently for me to read to them. They are so receptive to what I have to say in this window of time. They are also happier children for the next few days!

If your kids are older, I believe they will still find it special for you to invite them over, one-on-one, and love on them in the way you know best. I don't care how old we are. We never tire of parental love. My mother has found little ways to bless me even though I live out of state. She prepares special things for me when I come home to visit. And she will always try to make time for coffee on her beautiful front porch, just the two of us. It's in those spaces that the pain feels lighter, the struggle feels easier, and God's presence feels stronger. God meant for us to feel His love through other people. Whenever I own this truth, it keeps my mothering in perspective.

BACON BRUSSELS SPROUTS

If I am preparing a main course that is not exactly a family favorite, I like to make this side dish because everyone in my family loves "Bacon Brussels!"

3 cups brussels sprouts

¼ lb. bacon (about 4 slices)

1 tsp. garlic, minced

Salt and pepper to taste

Wash the brussels sprouts, cut them into quarters, and set aside. Cut the bacon into quarter-inch strips. Fry in a skillet for 6 to 8 minutes or until crispy. Remove the bacon from the pan using a slotted spoon and set aside.

Put brussels sprouts into the skillet with the bacon grease. Fry for 12 to 15 minutes, stirring occasionally. Return the bacon to the skillet. Add the garlic and fry for 1 minute. Turn off the heat and season with salt and pepper.

Serves 4 to 6

BOUNTIFUL HARVEST SALAD

I love the colors of fall. God is creative, and I love how He imparts creativity to each one of us. I learn so much from my friends. They spark creativity in me as I watch how they dress, decorate, and present food, and how they love God and others. It's so beautiful to me how even a salad can pack in many vibrant colors, and you can vary colors and flavors by using more or less of the ingredients. You can be super-creative with this one!

1 to 2 bunches Romaine lettuce, washed and chopped

¼ cup dates, chopped (look for these in your grocery store's produce section)

1 small bunch green onions (green parts included), diced

¼ cup pomegranate arils

½ cup corn, drained

½ cup sharp cheddar cheese, shredded

½ cup feta or goat cheese, crumbled

¼ cup tomatoes, diced

¼ cup pine nuts or salted sunflower seeds

¼ cup sliced almonds, or walnuts or pecans, chopped

1 red pear, unpeeled and thinly sliced

Vinaigrette dressing of your choice (this salad is great with the Apple Cider Vinaigrette Dressing on page 27)

Spread the lettuce over a 9 x 13-inch serving platter, leaving room around the outer edges. Start arranging the salad by placing the dates in a two-inch square, going from the outside in. Arrange the onions beside the dates, keeping them along the edge of the platter. Repeat with all of the remaining items. If you run out of ingredients before you make it all around the platter, fill the void with more of any of the items listed above.

Serving a salad this way is more than just pretty. It allows diners to choose the items they want on their lettuce.

Serves 8 to 10

HOMESTYLE HINT

*You can make this salad into a complete
meal by adding some grilled chicken.*

BUTTERSCOTCH APPLE SALAD

4 cups apples, washed and diced (a variety of red and green make this salad pretty—4 cups of apples equals 3 or 4 apples, depending on their size)

1 cup mini marshmallows

½ cup walnuts, chopped

2 cups whipping cream

1 small box (1.85 oz.) instant butterscotch pudding

2 T. brown sugar

Dice the apples and combine with the marshmallows and walnuts. Beat whipping cream until very soft peaks form. Add the pudding and brown sugar. Mix quickly and immediately add to apple mixture.

If your whipped cream/pudding mixture is too thick, add more unwhipped cream or a bit of milk. (The instant pudding makes this pudding mixture thicken really fast, so don't worry if it seems too thick. You haven't ruined your salad. We can assure you of that.)

Serves about 12

CINNAMON RED HOTS APPLESAUCE

This applesauce is pretty if put into a Jell-O mold and then at serving time unmolded on a plate with the center filled with cottage cheese.

⅔ cup red hot cinnamon candies

2 (3 oz.) pkgs. cherry Jell-O

2 cups boiling water

4 cups applesauce

Dissolve the candies in the boiling water (simmering in a saucepan on the stove is helpful). Dissolve the Jell-O in the same mixture. Add the applesauce and mix well. Pour into a bowl or mold and put in the refrigerator until set.

Yields 10 (5 oz.) servings

COOKED APPLES

This recipe is so simple, yet it shouts FALL in big, bold letters. I remember my grandmother serving these apples as a side dish in the place of applesauce. They are a great addition for a brunch alongside a breakfast casserole or a quiche.

The memories I have of my grandmother are of her either in her kitchen (and always wearing an apron) or in her garden. It didn't matter whether our visit was a planned event or we just popped in on a Saturday—she always had something delicious to offer us.

6 apples, cored, peeled, and sliced

¼ cup brown sugar

2 tsp. ground cinnamon

In a saucepan, put in enough water to cover the bottom of the pan. Then add the apples, brown sugar, and cinnamon; put on the lid. Cook over medium heat until soft, about 15 minutes. Stir and serve warm.

Serves 6

CRANBERRY WALDORF SALAD

 At our house, we enjoy cranberries in many forms—
including this light dish.

2 cups fresh cranberries

1 cup sugar

3 cups mini marshmallows

2 cups apples, chopped or grated

8 oz. pineapple tidbits, drained

1 cup grapes, halved

2 cups whipping cream

½ cup nuts, chopped (optional)

Wash the cranberries and blend them in a food processor
or blender until coarsely chopped. Add the sugar and allow
cranberries and sugar to set for 20 minutes.

During this time, combine marshmallows, apples, pineapple,
and grapes in a large bowl. Add the cranberries and sugar
mixture.

In a separate bowl, whip the cream until stiff peaks start to
form. Gently fold the whipped cream into the fruit mixture.
Chill for 2 hours before serving.

Yields approximately 12 cups

EASY-BAKE BUTTERNUT OR ACORN SQUASH

 This is an easy and delicious fall dish.

1 squash (figuring ½ per person)
2 T. butter
Salt and pepper to taste

Preheat the oven to 350°. Wash a squash and cut it in half. Scoop out the seeds. Grease a baking sheet and turn squash upside down on sheet. Bake for 45 to 60 minutes or until soft. Scoop out the pulp and serve with butter, salt, and pepper.

Serves 2

ROASTED POTATOES

This is one of our household's favorite side dishes. It is easy-peasy, and I can fill up on the sweet potatoes while watching my carb intake. My growing children, who need all the fuel they can get, can eat as much of this dish as they like. We have a large garden, and every year we plant at least 50 pounds of seed potatoes and quite a few slips of sweet potatoes. It's super fun to make this dish from our garden harvest.

This recipe makes a large amount of potatoes, so it's great for a party but can easily be broken down in half or even smaller.

   3 lbs. potatoes, washed and cubed

   3 to 4 large sweet potatoes, washed, peeled, and cubed

   ½ cup (1 stick) butter

   1 tsp. salt

   ¼ tsp. black pepper

   1 tsp. rosemary, dried

   1 tsp. garlic powder

   2 tsp. parsley, dried

   ⅛ tsp. red pepper flakes

Preheat the oven to 400°. Place the potato chunks on a large cookie sheet. Slice slivers of butter and spread them over the top of the potatoes. Sprinkle on all the spices. Place in the oven and bake, stirring the potatoes at the 10-minute mark. Bake, uncovered, for another 30 to 40 minutes, depending on how soft (or crispy) you like your potatoes.

Serves 12 to 14

HOMESTYLE HINT

Sweet potatoes can become too soft when baked for a long time. To avoid this, add the sweet potatoes at the 10-minute stirring mark noted above.

SAUSAGE GRAVY

2 lbs. bulk pork sausage

¼ cup butter

1¼ cups flour

8 cups milk

Salt and pepper to taste

1 tsp. soy sauce

Fry the sausage in butter until browned. Add the flour and stir well. Gradually add milk. Continue to heat (on low setting) and stir. The gravy will thicken as it cooks. If it gets too thick, add a little more milk. Add the seasonings. Serve over biscuits or potatoes.

Serves 8 to 10

SLOW-COOKER APPLE BUTTER

 This is such a fun fall thing to do. Not only is it delicious, but it also makes your kitchen smell good.

4 lbs. apples, peeled, cored, and sliced

1 cup apple cider

2 cups sugar

1 tsp. ground cinnamon

1 tsp. ground cloves

½ tsp. ground allspice

Place all the ingredients in a slow cooker and cook on low for 10 hours. (If you have too much liquid, remove the lid for the last 2 hours of cooking.)

Stir well. Ladle the hot apple butter into jars, leaving one-quarter inch of head space. Screw the lids on tightly and turn the jars upside down until cooled to seal. Refrigerate. For long-term storage, process the apple butter for 10 minutes in pint or half-pint jars using the water bath canning method.

Yields about 5 pt. jars

SWEET POTATO SOUFFLÉ

6 cups sweet potatoes, cooked and mashed

¼ cup brown sugar

1 tsp. salt

½ cup (1 stick) butter, melted

1 cup milk

2 eggs

CRUMB TOPPING

¾ cup brown sugar

⅔ cup flour

6 T. butter, melted

1½ cups pecans, chopped

Preheat the oven to 325°. Combine sweet potatoes, brown sugar, salt, butter, milk, and eggs. Place in an 8 x 11-inch baking dish. For the topping, combine the brown sugar, flour, butter, and pecans. Sprinkle the crumb topping over the sweet potato mixture. Bake for 30 minutes or until bubbly.

Serves 6 to 8

APPLE CRESCENTS

My daughter Jenelle introduced me to these fun and delicious dainties. I love it when my girls share new recipes with me. These sweet and fruity crescents are quite simple to make but look complex.

2 (8 oz.) cans refrigerated crescent rolls

¼ cup sugar

1 T. ground cinnamon

1 (20 oz.) can apple pie filling

¼ cup (½ stick) butter

Preheat the oven to 375°. Unroll the crescent rolls and separate into 16 triangles.

In a bowl, combine the sugar and cinnamon. Sprinkle one-half teaspoon of the cinnamon sugar on each triangle and then add 1 tablespoon of the pie filling. Roll up and place point side down on lightly greased baking sheet.

In a small saucepan, melt the butter. Drizzle the crescent rolls with the butter and remaining cinnamon sugar. Bake for 20 to 25 minutes or until golden brown. Serve warm and with a scoop of ice cream if desired.

Yields 16 fruit-filled crescent rolls

APPLE CRISP

FRUIT LAYER

4 cups apples, sliced

1 cup sugar

2 T. flour

1 tsp. cinnamon

Preheat the oven to 325°. In a bowl, mix the ingredients together and then place in a 9 x 13-inch pan.

CRUMB TOPPING

1¼ cups flour

1¼ cups oatmeal

¾ cup brown sugar

⅓ cup butter, melted

¼ tsp. baking soda

¼ tsp. baking powder

In another bowl, mix the topping ingredients together and put on top of apples. Bake for 30 minutes or until apples are soft. Serve warm with ice cream.

Serves 10

ENTERTAINING...THE HEART OF THE MATTER

It is so profound to me that Jesus says a cup of cold water given in His name is kingdom work. (See Mark 9:41.) We can so easily lose sight of the true heart of the matter when it comes to entertaining. We can get lost in the quest for a perfectly clean house, the perfectly decorated table, and the grandest feast. That's when Jesus pulls us back and says, *What really is important? How can you best represent Me to your guests? How can you pull this off with a genuine heart of humility?*

These questions are hard to answer at times. We want it all: a clean house, a perfect table, mannerly kids, and a bang-up meal. But we need to extend ourselves a little grace. If a friend of yours pulls off the perfect meal, bless her and enjoy the work of her hands.

But do not place those same expectations on yourself. The heart of the matter is this: Will your guests feel loved through being in your home? Did you serve them from a place of peace, or did you overstrive? At times like these, we can all carry unnecessary burdens. The meal you serve doesn't have to be a perfect, ready-for-Pinterest feast. It doesn't have to compete with some dinner a friend pulled off.

Jesus brings us back to that simple cup of cold water. If you serve your guests your simplest meal with a heart of love, then you're doing kingdom work. And remember, water is simple and inexpensive, but it's vital for life.

BUTTERSCOTCH CREAM PIE

 This recipe could also be called Salted Caramel Deliciousness!

⅔ cup flour

2 cups brown sugar

½ tsp. salt

4 cups milk

2 eggs

4 T. salted butter

½ tsp. vanilla

1 (9-inch) baked pie shell

1 cup whipping cream

¼ tsp. powdered sugar

1 tsp. vanilla

In a saucepan, whisk together the flour, brown sugar, salt, and milk. Cook over medium-high heat.

While this mixture heats up, beat the eggs in a large coffee cup or glass bowl. (I like to use a whisk or fork for this task.) Continue cooking the flour mixture on medium-high heat, stirring constantly, for 8 to 10 minutes, or until thickened. Remove from heat and add 1 cup of the hot mixture to your eggs. (This makes for a smoother filling than pouring the beaten eggs into the hot saucepan. This technique tempers the eggs with just the right amount of the hot pudding mixture.) Stir thoroughly. Now you can add the egg mixture to the saucepan.

Return the saucepan to the stovetop and heat for about 2 minutes or until it just begins to boil. Remove from heat and add the butter and vanilla. Allow to cool for a few minutes, and then place a piece of *heat-resistant* plastic wrap directly on top of the cooked mixture. This prevents the pudding from forming a thick crust on top. Place the filling in the refrigerator and chill for at least 4 hours.

When you're ready to serve, remove the cooled filling from the refrigerator and pour it into the pie shell. Beat the whipping cream just until soft peaks start to form. Add the powdered sugar and vanilla and beat a bit more, until mixed thoroughly. Top the pie with whipped cream and enjoy!

Serves 6 to 8

HOMESTYLE HINT

This filling tastes great in a graham cracker shell. You can also serve it in festive soufflé cups with no crust. The whipped cream, however, is a must.

CARAMEL CORN

2 cups brown sugar

1 cup (2 sticks) butter

½ cup light Karo syrup

½ tsp. baking soda

⅛ tsp. cream of tartar

1 tsp. vanilla

1 tsp. salt

32 cups (8 qt.) popped corn

In a saucepan, cook the brown sugar, butter, Karo syrup, baking soda, and cream of tartar for 5 minutes, stirring constantly. Remove from the heat and add the vanilla and salt.

Pour the caramel over the popcorn and stir well. Bake in a 14-quart stainless steel pan or roaster for 1 hour at 200°, stirring every 15 minutes.

Yields 32 cups caramel corn

LIGHT FROM THE DARKNESS

Meg Meeker, an author and pediatrician, has been giving me a lot of food for thought to ponder in the quiet places of my soul. In her book *The 10 Habits of Happy Mothers,* she writes, "Dark [as in depression] is dark, and it blinds those who live in its midst."* If you find there is a dark space in your soul as you're going about your day, maybe you need to take a nap, sit for 30 minutes with a cup of coffee, or call a friend. To press in when the darkness bears down on you won't make you stronger or buck up better.

I don't want to make light of chronic depression, but neither do I think we should overlook dark days in our own lives when they come. We should emerge from our times of darkness with softer hearts. Yes, the hard stuff will still be present when you awake from your nap. The cookies won't be baked, and the laundry won't be folded. However, your soul will have received some rest. As a young mom, I am learning to offer myself grace and to let some tasks go undone if that means I can face my husband and my kids with a little more patience on a given evening.

And on those days when we know about God's presence in our heads but don't feel it in our hearts, we must rest in the fact that Jesus, if we allow Him, can enter the darkest places of our souls. We can make a conscious decision to allow His light to shine the brightest however He may choose to show up in our life.

---

* Meg Meeker, *The 10 Habits of Happy Mothers* (New York, NY: Ballantine Books, 2011), 204.

DATE PUDDING

I learned to make this delicious dessert from my mother. It was always her assigned dish to take to family Christmas gatherings. She would layer it to almost overflowing in a big cut-glass bowl—and she would always bring her bowl home empty.

My mother usually topped her date pudding with sliced bananas. I like mine topped with caramel sauce.

CAKE

  1 cup dates, chopped

  1 T. butter

  1 tsp. baking soda

  1 cup boiling water

  1 egg, beaten

  1 tsp. vanilla

  ¼ tsp. salt

  1 cup sugar

  1 cup flour

Preheat the oven to 350°. Place the dates, butter, and soda in a bowl and then pour the boiling water over them. Mix well and let cool. Combine the rest of the cake ingredients into the date mixture. Pour the batter into a 9 x 13-inch baking dish and bake for 25 minutes. Let cool.

CARAMEL SAUCE

- 3 cups brown sugar
- 4½ cups water, divided
- 5 T. butter
- ¼ tsp. baking soda
- ¾ cup Clear Jel
- 2 tsp. vanilla
- 2 tsp. pure maple syrup (or maple flavoring)
- 4 cups whipping cream, whipped

Mix the brown sugar, 4 cups water, butter, and baking soda in a sauce pan and bring to a boil for 20 minutes. Mix the Clear Jel with the remaining half cup water and add to the sauce. Cook until thickened. Remove from heat and add the vanilla and maple syrup. Let cool.

In a separate bowl, whip the cream and set aside.

To assemble, cut the cake into cubes. In a pretty glass bowl, layer half the cake, half the sauce, and half the whipped cream. Repeat the layers. Serve chilled.

Serves 20

FRESH APPLE BARS WITH CINNAMON CREAM CHEESE FROSTING

APPLE BARS

    2 cups apples, shredded (2 to 4 apples)

    1 cup sugar

    1 cup olive oil

    3 eggs

    2½ cups flour

    ½ tsp. salt

    1 tsp. baking soda

    1 tsp. cinnamon

Preheat the oven to 350°. Wash, peel, and shred the apples. Set aside. Beat together the sugar and olive oil. Add the eggs and mix. Stir in the flour, salt, baking soda, and cinnamon. Pour into a 9 x 13-inch pan and bake for about 25 minutes or until inserted toothpick comes out clean.

CINNAMON CREAM CHEESE FROSTING

    8 oz. cream cheese, room temperature

    3 cups powdered sugar

    1 tsp. vanilla

    ½ tsp. cinnamon

    ¼ tsp. salt

Beat the cream cheese on high until creamy. Add the powdered sugar, vanilla, cinnamon, and salt. Mix completely and spread on the cooled apple bars.

Serves 12 to 16

GOOD MORNING MUFFINS

3 eggs

1 cup (2 sticks) butter, room temperature

1½ cups raw sugar

1 tsp. salt

2 tsp. vanilla

2 tsp. cinnamon

2 cups carrots, grated

1 cup apple, grated

2 scant cups flour

2 tsp. baking powder

½ cup raisins (optional)

½ cup chopped nuts (optional)

Preheat the oven to 350°. Place the eggs, butter, and sugar in a mixing bowl and beat well. Add the salt, vanilla, cinnamon, carrots, apple, flour, baking powder, and raisins and nuts if using. Mix just until blended. Place in muffin pans and bake for 16 to 18 minutes or until an inserted toothpick comes out clean.

Yields 18 to 20 muffins

HOMESTYLE HINT

You can easily make a drizzle out of powdered sugar and a tiny bit of cream to make these muffins extra pretty. Just mix the powdered sugar and cream in a cup until you get the pourable consistency you desire. Crisscross the drizzle over the top of the muffins.

HOT APPLE CIDER

 This is a cozy and delicious beverage for a fall party!

2 qt. apple cider (you can use apple juice, but its flavor is not as robust)

1½ qt. cranberry juice

2 cups water

½ cup brown sugar

1 tsp. whole cloves

1 tsp. whole allspice

3 cinnamon sticks

1 coffee filter

In a large kettle, combine the apple cider, cranberry juice, water, and brown sugar. Place the cloves, allspice, and cinnamon sticks in a coffee filter. Tie the filter closed with a string and place it in the liquid. Simmer over medium-high heat for 30 minutes.

Yields 16 cups

PUMPKIN BARS WITH CREAM CHEESE ICING

PUMPKIN BARS

4 eggs, beaten

2 tsp. cinnamon

1 cup vegetable oil

1 tsp. baking soda

2 cups sugar

1 tsp. baking powder

1 cup pumpkin puree

2 cups flour

½ tsp. salt

Preheat the oven to 350°. Combine all ingredients and spread onto a large baking sheet. Bake for 20 minutes. Allow to cool slightly.

CREAM CHEESE ICING

8 oz. cream cheese, softened

3½ cups powdered sugar

6 T. butter

2 T. milk

1 tsp. cinnamon

Cream together the cream cheese, powdered sugar, butter, and milk. Spread the icing over warm bars and then sprinkle with the cinnamon.

Serves 20

PUMPKIN COOKIES WITH MAPLE CREAM CHEESE FROSTING

These cookies don't require as much sugar as some other varieties do. They are also great without the maple cream cheese frosting listed below, but oh, the frosting is so delicious!

PUMPKIN COOKIES

- 1 cup (2 sticks) butter, room temperature
- 1 cup Sucanat or brown sugar
- 1 cup pumpkin puree
- 2 eggs
- 1 tsp. vanilla
- 1 tsp. baking powder
- ¼ tsp. sea salt
- 1½ tsp. cinnamon
- 2¼ cups flour

Preheat the oven to 350°. Combine the butter, Sucanat or sugar, pumpkin, eggs, and vanilla. Add the baking powder, salt, cinnamon, and flour. Stir until just mixed. Drop the dough using a small ice cream scoop onto a cookie sheet and flatten the cookies with the back of the scoop. Bake for 8 to 10 minutes. Frost if desired.

MAPLE CREAM CHEESE FROSTING

This recipe makes a lot of frosting. If you prefer only a thin layer on your cookies, you can halve the amount of the ingredients.

    8 oz. cream cheese, room temperature

    3 cups powdered sugar

    2 T. whipping cream

    1 tsp. maple flavoring

    ¼ tsp. salt

Beat the cream cheese until smooth. Add the powdered sugar, cream, maple flavoring, and salt. Blend until creamy. Frost cookies.

Yields 2½ to 3 dozen cookies

PUMPKIN DIP

 This is a fun addition to any fall party!

8 oz. cream cheese

¾ cup brown sugar

1 cup pumpkin puree

1 to 1½ tsp. cinnamon

Beat the cream cheese and brown sugar together. Add the pumpkin and cinnamon. Place in a serving bowl and sprinkle with a pinch of cinnamon. Refrigerate for 1 hour. Yields 2 cups. This is a wonderful dip for ginger snaps, apple slices, or graham crackers.

Serves 4 to 6

PUMPKIN GRANOLA BALLS

These little pumpkin balls are a great source of protein for growing children, and they pack a punch of sweetness that any pumpkin lover will enjoy.

1 cup pumpkin puree

½ cup almond or peanut butter

⅓ cup Sucanat or honey

2 tsp. cinnamon

½ tsp. salt

½ cup flax seed, ground

⅓ cup rolled oats

½ cup pumpkin seeds

½ cup pecan pieces

½ cup sunflower seeds, salted

½ cup chocolate chips

With a hand mixer, combine the pumpkin, almond butter or peanut butter, Sucanat or honey, cinnamon, and salt in a small bowl. Add the flax and oats and mix well.

In another small bowl, combine the pumpkin seeds, pecan pieces, sunflowers seeds, and chocolate chips. With a small cookie scoop, place half of a scoop of the pumpkin mixture into the seed/chocolate mixture. Roll until completely coated. Store in the refrigerator. You can also freeze half of them for a later date.

Yields 36

PUMPKIN MUFFINS

This yummy recipe is sweetened with honey and apple cider. My husband and his brother hand-press apple cider every December. Our young boys (ages 7 and 8) look forward to Apple Cider Day, when they travel to Uncle Chester's. Using a press that is a family heirloom, they can press between 160 and 180 gallons of cider—in one day. This is a tradition I know we will keep treasuring for years to come. Traditions like this are little gifts we give our children and ourselves. We freeze gallons of this sweet treat so that we can enjoy it throughout the winter, served with fresh popcorn by the fire.

2 eggs

½ cup (1 stick) butter, room temperature

½ cup honey

½ cup apple cider (or apple juice)

1 cup pumpkin puree

2 tsp. vanilla

½ tsp. salt

2 tsp. cinnamon

2 tsp. baking powder

1½ cups flour

½ cup old-fashioned oatmeal

½ cup walnuts, chopped

Preheat the oven to 350°. Beat together eggs, butter, honey, apple cider, and pumpkin puree. Add vanilla, salt, cinnamon, baking powder, flour, oats, and walnuts. Mix just until stirred together (the batter will be lumpy). Scoop into muffin pan liners. Bake for 15 to 18 minutes or until an inserted toothpick comes out clean.

Yields 18 muffins

WINTER

MAIN DISHES
Baked Beef Brisket 🌿

🌿 Barbecue Meatballs

🌿 Chicken Enchiladas

Chicken Fried Rice 🌿

🌿 Chicken Noodle Casserole

Chicken Tetrazzini 🌿

🌿 Crock-Pot Oatmeal

🌿 Garlic Shrimp Alfredo Bake

Golden Chicken Noodle or Chicken Rice Soup 🌿

Pizza Casserole 🌿

🌿 Rice Taco in a Skillet

Simple Fried Cod 🌿

🌿 Slow-Cooker Philly Steak Sandwiches

SAUCES, SIDE DISHES, AND SALADS
Artisan Bread with Pizza Crust Option 🌿

Avocado Salad Dressing 🌿

Baked Brown Rice 🌿

Cheese Garlic Biscuits 🌿

Cheese Platter 🌿

🌿 English Muffin Bread

🌿 French Dressing for Salads

🌿 Mustard Dip

🌿 Roasted Broccoli

Dawn's recipes are marked with a 🌿, and Carol's with a 🌿.

Taco Dip

Tortilla Chip Dip

Winter Salad with Lemon Dressing

SNACKS AND DESSERTS

Buckeyes

Butterscotch Pudding

Caramel Pineapple Rings

Cherry Delight

Cinnamon Nut Granola

Easy Gingerbread

Jelly Roll

Mini Snickerdoodle Cookie Cups with
Cinnamon Buttercream Frosting

Mint Cream Cheese Bars

Orange Drop Cookies with Frosting

Oreo Truffles

Peanut Butter Fingers

Peppermint Angel Cake Roll

Rosemary-Spiced Baked Nuts

Snow Cream

Sour Cream Coffee Cake with Crumb Topping

Turtle Cake

Upside-Down Date Pudding

Wonderful Simple Caramels

Dawn's recipes are marked with a 🌿 , and Carol's with a 🌾 .

Winter is such a beautiful season. It gives me permission to pause, to rest, to breathe. And I mean breathe *deeply*. Cold sets in, and all I want to do is cozy up under a blanket and rest. Just as the ground is resting, my soul needs rest. This is why I like WINTER!

BAKED BEEF BRISKET

My husband frequently travels to Texas on business. He has always talked about the brisket they serve down there, and he makes sure to have some on every trip at those roadside BBQ joints Texas is famous for.

Several years ago, our whole family was able to accompany him, and we spent more than three weeks in the Lone Star State. We learned to love brisket as much as Merv does. In fact, we visited one last BBQ shack before we drove across the state line on the way home. After that, brisket became a family favorite, especially on birthdays and holidays. The key to a good brisket is a very slow roast in a baking dish with a lid.

5½ to 6 lbs. beef brisket	1 large onion, sliced
2 to 3 T. liquid smoke	Salt and pepper to taste
12 to 16 garlic cloves, sliced	1½ cups water

Take several large sheets of aluminum foil and overlap them on your countertop. Place your brisket on the foil and drizzle with 1½ tablespoons of the liquid smoke. Add half of the garlic and onions, and then heavily salt and pepper it. Turn your brisket over and repeat the process. (I recommend baking the brisket with the fat side up.)

Once the brisket is seasoned on both sides, pour a half cup of water on it and then wrap tightly in foil. Double wrap it in foil, place the foiled meat in your baking dish, and pour in the remaining cup of water. Put the lid on your dish and bake at 200° for 4 to 6 hours. I like to check my brisket at the 5-hour mark, but if your meat is closer to 5 pounds than 6, check at the 4-hour mark.

Allow the meat to cool. Slice it against the grain and return it to the pan. If you are serving the brisket right away, just reheat with the pan juices. Remember, you want to *reheat*, not rebake. Serve with barbecue sauce if desired.

Serves about 12

BARBECUE MEATBALLS

MEATBALLS

3 lbs. ground beef (or 1½ lbs. ground beef and 1½ lbs. ground pork)

1 cup oatmeal

1 cup cracker crumbs

½ cup onion, chopped

1 (12 oz.) can evaporated milk

2 eggs

2 tsp. salt

½ tsp. pepper

½ tsp. garlic powder

2 tsp. chili powder

In a large bowl, combine the ingredients together and form into balls (an ice cream scoop works well for this). Place the meatballs into a 9 x 13-inch baking dish.

SAUCE

2 cups ketchup

½ tsp. liquid smoke (optional but good)

1 cup brown sugar

½ tsp. garlic powder

¼ cup onion, chopped

Mix the sauce ingredients together and pour over the meatballs. Bake at 350° for 1 hour.

Makes approximately 24 meatballs

HOMESTYLE HINT

Place the meatballs on a cookie sheet lined with wax paper and set it in the freezer. Once the meatballs are frozen, you can transfer them to freezer bags until you are ready to use them.

CHICKEN ENCHILADAS

1 pint sour cream

12 oz. cheddar cheese

1 cup salsa

Small onion, chopped

2 cups chicken, cooked and shredded

12 flour tortillas

Preheat the oven to at 350°. Combine the sour cream, cheese, salsa, onion, and cooked chicken. Put a large spoonful of the chicken mixture in the middle of each tortilla. Roll the tortillas and place folded-side-down into a baking dish. Pour any leftover sauce over tortillas and sprinkle more cheese over top. Bake for 25 minutes.

Serve with additional salsa.

Serves 12

CHICKEN FRIED RICE

This quick one-dish meal works so well for our family. It's one of our son Camden's favorites. It works well as long as I remember to put the rice in the cooker in the morning (so it has time to cool) and get the chicken out of the freezer. This recipe doesn't require a lot of prep time, but if I'm in a super-duper hurry, I run the onions, carrots, pepper, and garlic through my food processor so there is less chopping to do.

3 to 4 cups cooked rice (*cooled* rice works best)

2 T. coconut oil or butter

1 onion, chopped (about 1½ cups)

1 large carrot, diced

1½ lbs. chicken breast, diced

1 red pepper, diced

5 garlic cloves, minced

3 eggs, whisked together

4 green onions, diced, with greens on

⅛ to ¼ cup Bragg Liquid Aminos or soy sauce

Salt to taste (optional)

Several dashes of fish sauce (optional)

1 T. oyster sauce (optional)

Sunflowers seeds and extra green onions, for garnish

Heat the coconut oil in a skillet on medium-high setting. Add the onion and carrots and sauté for 3 to 5 minutes. Add the chicken and cook for 3 minutes. Add the pepper and garlic and cook for about 5 more minutes. Add the rice, stirring completely. Make a well in the center of your frying pan and add the beaten eggs and green onions. Allow the eggs to cook for 2 minutes, and then chop up the cooked eggs and stir the mixture completely until eggs are well fried. Add the soy sauce and the seasonings of your choice. Serve with sunflower seeds and green onions.

Serves 6 to 8

HOMESTYLE HINT

Look for fish sauce and oyster sauce in the international section of your local grocery store. They are common Asian sauces.

BONUS HOMESTYLE HINT

Triple-rinsing your rice will remove the starchy residue and make the rice less gummy. I put my rice in the rice-cooker bowl, rinse it with water, and then pour off the chalky water. I repeat the process twice more, and I am always amazed at how much starch washes off.

CHICKEN NOODLE CASSEROLE

1 (8 oz.) pkg. noodles

¾ lb. boneless, skinless chicken breasts, cubed

2 T. oil

½ cup butter, melted

⅓ cup flour

1 (10 oz.) cream of mushroom soup

2 cups chicken broth

4 oz. Havarti cheese

1 tsp. salt

½ tsp. pepper

½ cup Parmesan cheese

Preheat the oven to 350°.

Bring 5 cups of salted water to a boil and add the noodles. Cook until al dente, about 8 to 10 minutes. Drain and set aside.

While the noodles are boiling, heat the oil in a skillet and then add the chicken. Cook until done. Set aside.

In a large saucepan, melt the butter and then sprinkle on the flour; whisk together. When blended, stir in the soup and the chicken broth. Then add the Havarti cheese, noodles, chicken, and salt and pepper. Stir until combined well.

Transfer the chicken and noodle mixture to a greased 9 x 13-inch baking pan. Top with the Parmesan cheese and bake for 20 minutes.

Serves 10 to 12

CHICKEN TETRAZZINI

Sometimes you just need comfort food, particularly when the snow is falling. This dish takes me back to the farm where I grew up. I recall cooking for some hungry, hardworking farm boys—also known as my brothers. I am thankful that our creative God inspired me to develop a low-carb version of this dish featuring spaghetti squash if I want it.

- 16 oz. angel hair pasta, cooked al dente (or 6 or 7 cups baked spaghetti squash)
- 3 to 4 cups cooked chicken (rotisserie chicken works great!)
- 1 cup white American cheese, torn into small pieces
- 2½ cups chicken broth
- 12 oz. cream of chicken soup (I use Pacific Food's organic soup)
- 1 tsp. garlic powder
- 2 T. parsley, dried

Preheat the oven to 350°. Place the pasta or squash in a large bowl and add the chicken and cheese pieces. In a small bowl, combine chicken broth, chicken soup, garlic powder, and parsley, and then stir that into the pasta or squash mixture. Place in a 9 x 13-inch baking dish and bake for 45 minutes, covered.

Serves 10 to 12

HOMESTYLE HINT

While this is a hearty dish and easily feeds my family twice, don't rule this recipe out because it looks like too much food. It can be prepared and frozen before you bake it. Or if you don't like that option, halve the recipe.

CROCK-POT OATMEAL

 This is a wonderful recipe to use when you need a quick, on-the-go breakfast.

½ cup brown sugar

1 cup chopped apples

2 cups milk

½ cup Craisins

1 T. melted butter

¼ tsp. salt

1 tsp. cinnamon

1 cup old-fashioned oats

½ cup chopped walnuts (optional)

Grease your slow cooker, place all of the ingredients inside, and stir. Cover with the lid. Just before going to bed, turn your cooker setting to low. In the morning, you'll wake up to a breakfast that smells wonderful. Serve with milk.

Serves 5 to 6

GARLIC SHRIMP ALFREDO BAKE

10 oz. penne pasta

3 T. butter

3 cloves fresh garlic, minced

1 lb. large shrimp, thawed, deveined, and tails off

3 T. chopped fresh parsley (or 2 tsp. dried parsley flakes)

2 T. flour

¾ cup half-and-half (or whole milk)

¼ cup chicken broth

¼ cup plus 2 T. Parmesan cheese, shredded

1 cup mozzarella cheese, shredded

Freshly ground black pepper to taste

1 large tomato, diced (about 1 cup)

Preheat the oven to 350°.

Cook the pasta in 5 cups water, salted if desired, about 12 to 15 minutes. When it's al dente, drain and set aside.

In a skillet, melt 1 tablespoon of the butter. Add the garlic and the parsley and season with salt to taste. Cook the shrimp in the garlic mixture for 2 minutes on each side or until pink, and then transfer the shrimp to a plate. Keep the juices in the skillet and add the remaining 2 tablespoons of butter.

When the butter has melted, add the flour and whisk until nicely browned, about 1 to 2 minutes. Add half-and-half or milk and the chicken broth. Bring the liquid to a simmer, and then stir in three-fourths of the mozzarella cheese and the one-quarter cup of the Parmesan cheese till creamy. Season with freshly ground black pepper.

Return the shrimp to the skillet and add the chopped tomatoes and pasta. Toss. If the dish is too thick, add a bit more milk. Transfer the shrimp mixture to a 9 x 13-inch baking dish and sprinkle with remaining mozzarella and Parmesan cheeses. Bake for 20 minutes.

Serves 6 to 8

GOLDEN CHICKEN NOODLE OR CHICKEN RICE SOUP

Making your own chicken stock is one of the best things you can do for your family. I have chicken carcasses in my freezer just waiting for the day it's time to make stock. When any of us is sick, it's chicken soup time.

Stock is really easy to make, but I do get tired of the smell when I simmer it for 24 hours on my stovetop. So I like to simmer my stock in my large slow cooker in the basement.

1 cup onion, diced

2 T. butter

3 qt. (12 cups) chicken broth or stock

1 cup carrots, diced

1 cup celery, diced

4 cups chicken, diced and cooked (try using a rotisserie chicken or some leftover turkey)

4 cups rice, cooked, or 16 oz. noodles, cooked al dente

1 heaping tsp. turmeric (This is a key ingredient. Turmeric provides rich color and flavor, and it packs many health benefits as well.)

1 to 2 tsp. garlic, minced

½ to 1 tsp. salt (taste before adding)

½ tsp. black pepper

2 T. parsley, dried

In a large stock pot, sauté the onion in butter for 2 to 3 minutes. Add the broth or stock, carrots, and celery, and bring the mixture to a rolling boil. Simmer for 5 to 7 minutes. Add the chicken, rice or noodles, turmeric, garlic, salt, pepper, and parsley.

Yields 10-12 servings (If you have leftovers, this soup freezes well.)

HOMESTYLE HINT

You can cook the noodles with the broth mixture to save yourself some time—and a dirty kettle. Just be sure to follow the package directions because cooking times vary from pasta to pasta. By the way, if your pasta cooking time is longer than the 5 to 7 minutes allotted for the vegetables, that's no problem. Cooking the vegetables for a few extra minutes won't make your soup any less delicious!

BONUS HOMESTYLE HINT

If you're struggling to introduce brown rice to your family, this soup might be your solution. Brown rice absorbs flavors well, and you might find that your family members don't even realize they are eating something healthful. It's a win-win.

PIZZA CASSEROLE

This recipe easily provides two meals for my family of six. We enjoy one casserole on the night I prepare it, and I freeze the other for a later date. I love it when I can prepare two meals at one time—freeing up an afternoon down the road. Here's another time-saver: I often cook large quantities (4 to 6 pounds) of ground beef in my Crock-Pot. Once the meat is cooked, I chop it up and freeze it in 1- or 2-pound bags. (There is something about standing over a stove and frying meat night after night that feels like a waste of precious time to me.)

2 lbs. ground beef

16 oz. egg noodles

48 oz. pasta sauce

12 oz. mushroom soup

½ cup pepperoni

1 tsp. garlic powder

1 tsp. basil

1 tsp. oregano

1 cup Parmesan cheese, shredded

16 oz. mozzarella cheese, shredded

Preheat the oven to 350°. Fry the hamburger in a skillet (or use a slow cooker). Cook the noodles al dente per package instructions. Combine cooked hamburger and noodles in a large mixing bowl. Add the pasta sauce (rinse out the jar or can with ¼ cup water and add to the mixing bowl), mushroom soup, pepperoni, seasonings, and half of the shredded cheese and mix.

Divide into two casserole dishes. Freeze one for later and bake the other for 45 minutes. Top with the remaining cheese.

Serves 12 to 14

RICE TACO IN A SKILLET

1 lb. ground beef

2 garlic cloves, minced

1 (1¼ oz.) pkg. taco seasoning

8 oz. taco sauce

2 cups water

1 cup rice, uncooked

1 (16 oz.) can refried beans

2 cups cheddar cheese

1 (10 oz.) bag Doritos, crushed

Sour cream (optional)

Lettuce (optional)

Salsa (optional)

Fresh tomatoes (optional)

Onions, diced (optional)

In a skillet, brown the ground beef and garlic. Add the taco seasoning, taco sauce, water, and rice. Heat to boiling, and then turn down the heat and simmer on low for approximately 30 minutes (or until the rice is soft and has absorbed the liquid.)

Add the refried beans and cheddar cheese and stir well. Serve the meat and rice mixture over crushed Doritos, topping with sour cream, lettuce, and salsa if desired. Fresh tomatoes and diced onions are delicious as well.

Serves 6 to 8

SIMPLE FRIED COD

My friend Mrs. Bo, who is such a great cook, introduced me to a similar version of this cod. Then I tweaked it a bit to fit our liking. I hope you will find this recipe as delicious as we do. Sometimes you just need Friday night fish and chips, especially when the fish is nice and crisp and puffy.

2 to 3 lbs. cod, cut into fillets

Salt and pepper to taste

1 cup flour

1 tsp. Old Bay seasoning

Pinch of cayenne pepper

2 tsp. baking powder

¾ cup water

2 eggs, beaten

Approximately 2 to 3 cups coconut oil or your choice of oil for frying

Salt and pepper the fish on both sides. In a separate dish, stir together the flour, Old Bay, cayenne pepper, and baking powder. Add the water and eggs and mix well. Place several inches of oil in a skillet and set temperature to medium-high. (I like to get the oil to between 325° and 350° so the fish fries golden brown but not too quickly. It takes about 5 minutes for my oil to reach the right temperature.) Place the fish fillets in the batter and coat thoroughly. Fry in oil until golden brown, about 2 to 3 minutes per side. Place on a plate lined with paper towels. Serve immediately.

Serves 4 to 6

SLOW-COOKER PHILLY STEAK SANDWICHES

1½ lb. cube steaks

Salt and pepper to taste

Mushrooms, sliced (optional)

4 oz. cream cheese

1 cup provolone cheese

Onion, chopped, for garnish

4 deli buns (or 8 slices of bread)

Place one-quarter cup water in a slow cooker and add the raw steak one piece at a time.

Season with salt and pepper or seasonings of your choice. Repeat until all of the steaks have been seasoned. Place the cooker setting on low for 8 hours.

When the meat is cooked, shred it with two knives and then add the cream cheese and provolone. Stir until melted.

Serve the cheesesteak on toasted deli buns or toasted homemade bread. Top with onion. If you like mushrooms, they could be cooked with the steak and would make a nice additional topping.

Serves 4

ARTISAN BREAD WITH PIZZA CRUST OPTION

This crusty, European-style bread is a game-changer for those of us trying to manage our carbs and/or pair good, healthy carbs with protein. In order for this bread to have a lower carb index, you must mix the dough and let it refrigerate for three days before baking. (Some research indicates that the fermentation process can reduce the carb content.)

This dough works well even if refrigerated 7 or 8 days. And you can use half of this recipe to bake a loaf of bread for dinner, and then use the rest for a pizza crust later in the week.

I have had it sitting in my refrigerator for as many as 8 days before I used it, and it was fine.

One final note: A glass baking dish with a lid is essential for this recipe.

> 3 cups warm water
> 1½ T. sea salt
> 5½ cups white wheat flour
> 1½ T. instant yeast

In a large bowl, combine all the ingredients. Stir with a wooden spoon until everything is completely mixed. Place in a glass bowl and cover loosely with plastic wrap. Allow the dough to rise for two hours and then place in your refrigerator. After three days, pull off as much dough as you want for your loaf of bread and place on parchment paper.

Preheat your oven to 450°. After 20 minutes, place the glass baking dish, with lid, into your oven and let it heat for 20 minutes. When the time is up, remove the dish from the oven and place your bread dough inside. Put the lid back on and bake for 25 to 30 minutes. If you want a bit of a dark top, you can remove the lid for the last 10 minutes of the baking time.

Yields 2 loaves

HOMESTYLE HINT

This recipe makes great pizza dough. Just spread it on your pizza pan, add your favorite toppings, and bake in a preheated 400-degree oven for 18 to 20 minutes or until the cheese is bubbly. Here's another option: You can make focaccia bread using half of the recipe above. Spread the dough thin on a baking sheet. Sprinkle with one or two teaspoons of Dipping Herbs (see the recipe on page 24) and then drizzle two or three tablespoons of olive oil over the top. Bake at 350° for 12 to 14 minutes.

AVOCADO SALAD DRESSING

This is a rich, creamy, good-for-you salad dressing with no added sugar. It's great for anyone doing a sugar detox.

½ ripe avocado

¼ cup olive oil

2 T. apple cider vinegar

¼ cup onion, diced

¼ cup almonds, slivered

2 T. sunflower seeds

2 to 3 garlic cloves

1 cup water

½ tsp. Italian seasoning

½ tsp. sea salt

Pinch of black pepper

Half of a jalapeño pepper (optional)

Place all of the ingredients into a blender and mix until the dressing is pureed and smooth. Serve with the salad of your choice. Keeps in the refrigerator for one week.

Yields about 2 cups

BAKED BROWN RICE

Brown rice represents an ongoing struggle in our house. I like the fiber in it that helps with the carb count and the fact that it's packed with vitamins and minerals. But my family gives me such pushback. They would eat white jasmine rice every night if they could. (They even balk at *brown* jasmine rice.) This side dish recipe saves the day for me. The brown rice is so well disguised they hardly know it's there.

- 2 cups brown rice
- 32 oz. chicken or beef broth (depending on your choice of meat for the main course)
- 1 T. dried onion or 2 T. fresh minced onion
- 2 cloves garlic
- 1 T. parsley
- ½ tsp. salt
- 2 T. butter
- ½ tsp. turmeric (helps "disguise" the brown rice, and it provides antioxidant and anti-inflammatory benefits)

Soak the rice for 5 minutes and then rinse twice. Combine the rice, broth, onions, garlic, parsley, salt, butter, and turmeric in an ovenproof bowl with lid. Bake at 350° for 90 minutes. Let rest for 10 minutes before serving. Garnish with dried parsley if desired.

Serves 6 to 8

HOMESTYLE HINT

You can grate carrots into this rice dish to give it more color. Also, if you don't have a baking dish with a lid, you can use foil, but it won't seal in the moisture as well.

CHEESE GARLIC BISCUITS

 This is a low-carb recipe.

1 cup almond flour

½ cup coconut flour

1 T. baking powder

1 tsp. garlic powder

½ tsp. salt

1 cup Parmesan cheese

1 cup light cream

2 T. parsley

4 eggs

½ cup (1 stick) butter, room temperature

1½ cups cheddar cheese, shredded

Extra butter and parsley for drizzling on top of biscuits (optional)

Preheat the oven to 350°. In a medium bowl, combine the flours. Add the baking powder, garlic powder, salt, Parmesan cheese, cream, parsley, eggs, and butter. Blend with a hand mixer.

Stir the cheddar cheese into the mixture. With a cookie scoop, place the biscuits on a baking sheet. Bake for 16 to 18 minutes. Remove from the oven and drizzle with extra butter. Sprinkle with parsley, if desired. Serve warm.

Yields 2 dozen large biscuits

HOMESTYLE HINT

I like to bake just enough biscuits for a dinner or lunch because these are best warm. I store the rest of the dough in the fridge for a few nights so that we can enjoy fresh biscuits again without all the extra work. By the way, these biscuits pair well with soup.

BONUS HOMESTYLE HINT

As I seek to make wise food-related choices, I have found nutrition researcher Sally Fallon to be a reliable guide. I recommend her Nourishing Traditions series of books. I also recommend Sarah Pope's The Healthy Home Economist, thehealthyhomeeconomist.com, which offers a wealth of good information. Lastly, you might check out www.momsaware.org. Both of these websites have influenced me.

CHEESE PLATTER

8 to 12 oz. any three cheeses of your choice, sliced or cubed (I suggest white cheddar, marble, and one other)

Pecans or spiced pecans (see the recipe for Rosemary-Spiced Baked Nuts later in this section)

Dried apricots

1 pear or small bunch of red grapes

Fresh rosemary sprig or mint leaves

Place the cheeses on the corners of a large serving tray. Place the apricots in the middle of the tray and the pecans next to one of the cheeses. Cut the pear in half, take out the core, and then slice it very thin. Place skin-side up. If you have a cheese knife, place it on one of the blocks of cheese. You can also add variety by dicing the marble cheese into cubes and putting some toothpicks close by.

Serves 15 to 18

ENGLISH MUFFIN BREAD

This recipe is fun to bake in tin cans. Spray clean cans with Pam before adding the dough. Open just one end and bake vertically.

2 (¼ oz.) pkgs. yeast (do not dissolve in water)

1 T. sugar

2 tsp. salt

¼ tsp. baking soda

5½ to 6 cups flour, divided

2 cups milk

½ cup water

Cornmeal

Preheat the oven to 400°.

In a large bowl, combine the yeast, sugar, salt, and baking soda with 3 cups of the flour.

Heat the milk and water until very warm but not hot. Add the liquid to the dry ingredients and beat well. Stir in more flour to make a stiff batter, a half cup at a time.

Divide the dough into two bread pans that have been greased and sprinkled with cornmeal. Sprinkle the tops of the loaves with cornmeal. Cover and let rise in a warm place for 45 minutes.

Bake for 25 minutes. Remove the loaves from the bread pans immediately and let cool on wire racks.

Yields 2 loaves

FRENCH DRESSING FOR SALADS

¾ cup sugar

½ cup vinegar

1 cup ketchup

1½ cups olive oil

½ tsp. each paprika, celery seed, and onion salt

Simply mix the above ingredients in a blender and you're done!

Yields 3 cups

MUSTARD DIP

1½ cups mayonnaise (I suggest Hellman's)
¼ cup prepared mustard
½ cup honey

Combine all ingredients. Great for dipping chicken nuggets and pretzels (soft and hard). This dip is also a fine condiment for sandwiches.

Yields about 2¼ cups

ROASTED BROCCOLI

3 cups broccoli florets or broccoli/cauliflower mixed

4 T. butter, slivered

Salt, pepper, and granulated garlic to taste

Preheat the oven to 400°. Wash broccoli and cut into small florets. Place on a baking sheet and top with slivers of butter. Sprinkle with salt, pepper, and granulated garlic. Bake for 5 minutes, and then stir and bake another 5 minutes.

If you like your broccoli a bit crispier, stir a second time and bake for 5 minutes more (a total of 15 minutes baking time).

Serves 4

TACO DIP

8 oz. cream cheese

1 pkg. taco seasoning

½ cup sour cream

1 (10 oz.) can refried beans

1 cup lettuce, shredded

1 small tomato, diced

Small can black olives, sliced

3 green onions, snipped

1 cup cheddar cheese, shredded

Taco sauce for garnish

Mix together the cream cheese, taco seasoning, and sour cream. Spread on serving plate. Spread refried beans onto cream cheese layer. Next, layer the lettuce, tomato, olives, onions, and cheese. Garnish with the taco sauce. Serve with tortilla chips or crackers.

Yields 3 cups

TORTILLA CHIP DIP

2 lbs. hamburger

½ cup onion, chopped (optional)

1 (10.5 oz.) can cream of tomato soup

1 (10.5 oz.) can cheddar cheese soup

1 (10.5 oz.) can cream of mushroom soup

1 (16 oz.) jar salsa

Tortilla chips

In a skillet, brown the hamburger and the onion if using. Add the remaining ingredients, mix well, and simmer for 30 minutes. Serve immediately or keep warm in a slow cooker if serving later. Serve with tortilla chips.

Serves 10 to 12

WINTER SALAD WITH LEMON DRESSING

DRESSING

¾ cup olive oil

¼ cup fresh lemon juice

2 garlic cloves, minced

½ tsp. salt

½ tsp. pepper

SALAD

2 lbs. lettuce, diced

2 cups tomatoes or bell peppers, diced

1 cup Swiss cheese, shredded

1 cup slivered almonds, toasted

½ cup Parmesan cheese, shredded

½ lb. bacon, cooked and crumbled

¼ cup pomegranate arils (seed pods)

In a 1-cup mason jar, add the oil, lemon juice, garlic, salt, and pepper. Secure the jar lid and shake well.

Prepare salad on a large, flat serving platter, layering the lettuce, tomatoes, Swiss cheese, almonds, shredded Parmesan cheese, and bacon. Top with pomegranate arils. Pour the dressing over the salad when ready to serve.

Serves 12 to 14

BUCKEYES

I have fond memories of candy-making days with my mom and grandma. Buckeyes were always in the lineup. (These are sometimes called peanut butter balls, but I am from Ohio, so it's buckeyes for me.) My kids all love buckeyes, even though a couple of them thought they didn't like peanut butter.

2 cups salted peanut butter

1 cup (2 sticks) butter, room temperature

5 cups powdered sugar

¼ tsp. sea salt

4½ to 5 cups milk chocolate chips (you can use semisweet or dark chocolate if you choose)

Place peanut butter, butter, powdered sugar, and salt into a mixing bowl. Beat until thoroughly mixed. Using a small cookie scooper (or your hands), form balls about a half inch in diameter. Place on a cookie sheet lined with parchment paper. (You can refrigerate your buckeyes for 30 minutes to make them a bit more firm for dipping.)

In a double boiler, melt the chocolate chips on low heat, stirring often. Once completely melted, use a toothpick to dip the peanut butter balls into the chocolate. Cover *almost* completely so that the balls resemble a buckeye nut. Place back on parchment paper and allow to sit until hardened, about one hour. Store covered. Buckeyes will keep for about a month in the refrigerator, or 6 months in the freezer—if they last that long.

Yields approximately 95 to 100 balls

BUTTERSCOTCH PUDDING

4 T. butter

½ cup brown sugar

¾ cup flour

2 cups milk

3 egg yolks

1 tsp. vanilla

Melt and brown the butter in a medium-sized saucepan. Combine the brown sugar and flour, and then stir into the butter until blended. Whisk together milk and egg yolks. Stir into the butter mixture and cook over low heat, being sure to stir constantly until thickened. Remove from heat and stir in the vanilla.

When completely cooled, beat with a mixer until smooth.

Serves 4

CARAMEL PINEAPPLE RINGS

This treat is easy-peasy. If you love a good dessert but also love ease and convenience (as I do), this recipe could become one of your favorites. You will need a slow cooker for this one—and about 24 hours for the cooking and cooling process.

> 2 (14 oz.) cans sweetened condensed milk, labels removed (I recommend Eagle Brand, as I have had the best success with this one)
>
> 2 (15 oz.) cans pineapple rings, drained (or fresh pineapple cut into slices)
>
> 1 cup whipping cream
>
> ¼ cup powdered sugar
>
> Mint leaves and pomegranate arils (seed pods) for garnish

Place the *unopened* cans of sweetened condensed milk in a slow cooker. Fill the cooker with warm water until the cans are covered. Cook on low heat for 10 to 12 hours or until the milk becomes sliceable and caramel-like. (Cookers vary. One of my slow cookers needs 10 hours; the other one needs 12.) I like to cook the milk overnight. When you're ready to prepare the dessert, open the cans at both ends with a can opener. Use a dinner knife (run warm water over it) to go all around the outside of the caramelized milk, and then push it onto a cutting board.

Open the cans of pineapple slices and drain. Set the pineapple on a paper towel to absorb more of the juices, as this will help the caramel to sit nicely on the fruit. Cut the caramel into 9 to 10 slices. Place the pineapple rings on a serving tray and top with the caramel slices. Beat the whipping cream until soft peaks start to form. Add powdered sugar and mix until stiff peaks form. Top each pineapple ring with a hearty dab of whipping cream. Garnish with a mint leaf and 1 to 2 pomegranate arils. Serve immediately.

Yields 18 to 20 desserts

HOMESTYLE HINT

You can slow cook several cans of sweetened condensed milk at one time and then refrigerate some of them for later use. A can of cooked milk will keep for months if it's unopened in the fridge. By the way, if ever a can of milk doesn't set up properly, it can still make a delicious caramel dipping sauce for apples or other fruit.

CHERRY DELIGHT

 This is a dessert that is relatively easy to make and always seems to be enjoyed by young and old.

CRUST

½ cup (1 stick) butter, melted

1½ cups crushed graham crackers

Combine the two ingredients and spread into a 9 x 13-inch pan.

TOPPING

2 (8 oz.) pkg. cream cheese, softened

1 cup whipping cream

½ cup powdered sugar

1 tsp. vanilla

2 (21 oz.) cans of pie filling (I like Thank You brand)

Beat the cream cheese, and then add the whipping cream, powdered sugar, and vanilla. Beat for at least 5 minutes. Spread over graham cracker crust. Refrigerate until set. Top with your choice of fruit filling. One of our favorites is cherry pie filling. Peach and blueberry are also delightful. Or you can change things up by using just one can of pie filling and one cup each of blackberries, raspberries, and blueberries.

Yields 15 servings

CINNAMON NUT GRANOLA

12 cups rolled oats (*not* instant)

1½ cups unsweetened shredded coconut

3 cups walnuts or pecans, chopped

1 cup flax, ground

1 cup (2 sticks) butter

1 cup coconut oil (or oil of your choice)

2 tsp. salt

2 T. cinnamon

½ cup Sucanat or brown sugar

1½ cups honey

2 tsp. vanilla

Preheat the oven to 275°. In a large bowl, combine oats, coconut, nuts, and flax.

In a saucepan, melt butter and coconut oil. Remove from heat and add the salt, cinnamon, Sucanat or sugar, honey, and vanilla. Stir well. Add this to dry mixture and combine thoroughly.

Divide the granola onto two jelly roll pans. (I recommend lining the pans with parchment for easier cleanup.) Bake uncovered for 45 to 60 minutes, until golden brown. Stir every 20 minutes.

Yields 18 cups

EASY GINGERBREAD

½ cup (1 stick) butter

1 cup molasses

1 cup buttermilk

1 tsp. baking soda, dissolved in the buttermilk

2 eggs

1 cup sugar

2½ cups flour

1 tsp. cinnamon

1 tsp. ground ginger

Preheat oven to 350°. Combine all ingredients in a bowl and beat for 3 minutes. Bake in an 8 x 8-inch greased pan for 30 to 40 minutes.

Serve warm with whipped cream or Butterscotch Pudding (see recipe on page 187).

Yields 9 servings

JELLY ROLL

This is actually a cake roll, and I remember it as a popular dessert while growing up. Not sure why it's called a jelly roll, unless it used to be filled with jelly and rerolled.

BATTER

4 eggs

¾ cup sugar

¾ cup flour

¾ tsp. baking powder

¼ tsp. salt

1 tsp. vanilla

Preheat the oven to 400°. Beat the eggs until light and fluffy, about 5 minutes. Add the sugar, flour, baking powder, salt, and vanilla.

Line a jelly roll pan with wax or parchment paper sprayed with oil or nonstick spray. Pour the batter over the top. Bake for 12 minutes.

While the cake is baking, dust a dish towel with powdered sugar. After the cake has baked, flip upside down onto the towel. Roll the cake and towel together, starting from the short side. Allow to cool completely before adding the filling.

FILLING

4 oz. cream cheese

1 cup whipped cream, sweetened

1 tsp. vanilla

Cream the cream cheese, adding whipped cream and vanilla. Unroll the cake and spread the filling. Add sliced or chopped strawberries, if desired, and reroll. Slice and serve.

Yields 12 servings

MINI SNICKERDOODLE COOKIE CUPS WITH CINNAMON BUTTERCREAM FROSTING

Our all-time favorite grocery store, Wegmans, sells a large version of these cookie cups. This recipe allows for a lot of buttercream frosting—maybe too much for our own good. But, oh my, it's like a party in your mouth! These great little treats are perfect for any occasion.

COOKIE DOUGH

1 cup (1 stick) butter, room temperature

1½ cups sugar

2 eggs

2¾ cups flour

2 tsp. cream of tartar

1 tsp. baking soda

½ tsp. salt

3 T. sugar

3 tsp. cinnamon

CINNAMON BUTTERCREAM FROSTING

1½ cups (3 sticks) butter, room temperature

1½ tsp. vanilla

1½ T. cinnamon

3 cups powdered sugar

¼ cup + 1 T. whipping cream

Preheat oven to 350°. Combine the butter, sugar, and eggs. Add the flour, cream of tartar, baking soda, and salt.

In a small bowl, combine the cinnamon and sugar. With a small cookie scoop, drop the dough balls into the cinnamon-sugar mixture. Place the balls in a small mini muffin pan.

Press down in the centers with your thumb to make a deep indention. Bake for 7 to 9 minutes.

While the dough is baking, put together the frosting. Mix the butter, vanilla, cinnamon, powdered sugar, and whipping cream with a hand mixer.

When the cookie cups have cooled completely, drop 1 to 2 teaspoons of frosting on top of each one. You can also use a cake-decorating tip to pipe frosting onto the cookies. Be sure to brew a fresh pot of coffee when you enjoy these, as they *require* coffee!

Yields 60 little muffin cookies

MINT CREAM CHEESE BARS

4 (1 oz.) squares unsweetened baking chocolate

½ cup (1 stick) plus 2 T. butter, divided

2 cups sugar

4 eggs, divided

2 tsp. vanilla

1 cup flour

8 oz. cream cheese, softened

1 T. cornstarch

1 (14 oz.) can sweetened condensed milk

1 tsp. peppermint flavoring

1 cup semisweet chocolate chips

½ cup cream

Preheat the oven to 350°. Melt the baking chocolate and one stick butter in a saucepan. Stir until smooth.

In a separate bowl, combine the sugar, 3 eggs, vanilla, and flour in a large bowl. Add the chocolate mixture. Blend well.

Spread into a greased 9 x 13-inch baking pan and bake for 10 to 12 minutes.

Meanwhile, in a medium-size bowl, beat together the cream cheese, cornstarch, and remaining 2 tablespoons of butter until light and fluffy. Gradually beat in the sweetened condensed milk, peppermint flavoring, and remaining egg.

Pour over the hot cake layer. Bake for 30 minutes or until set.

Next, combine chocolate chips and cream in a small saucepan. Cook over low heat until smooth, being careful to stir constantly. Spread over the mint layer, let cool, and refrigerate until set. Cut into bars.

Makes 3 dozen

HOMESTYLE HINT

These refreshing bars make a festive Christmas treat. If you want to, add a drop or two of green food coloring to the cream cheese mixture and then garnish the tops with crushed candy canes. They also look nice without the food coloring and the crushed candy canes.

ORANGE DROP COOKIES WITH FROSTING

My maternal grandmother died at the young age of 56, when I was only 12. She was a very giving person who loved hospitality. I have great memories of her. Yes, I wish we would have had more days with her, but I am thankful for the good gifts she gave me in the short time she was here on this earth. Her home was always open and welcoming. I remember having my first orange drop cookie at her house.

The small things in life really matter. They strengthen our souls. For example, this is just a simple cookie recipe, but it evokes so much more. It reminds me of a place where I was loved and hugged, a place where family traditions were forged. I recall my grandfather praying and reading Scripture to us at bedtime when I stayed at their house. I remember how we were always served our favorite Schwan's ice cream at the holidays, and how we enjoyed orange push-pops on hot summer days. These are simple things, but they helped lay a foundation for my soul—and it started with filling my little tummy.

I believe God regards food as a big part of creating *home*—that place we always long for. So I share this special family recipe with you. I hope it inspires you to think about the ways you can create a sense of home for the people you love. These cookies won't evoke the same emotions for you as they do for me, but think about some food or a special recipe you grew up with that does it for you and take the time to introduce your family to it.

COOKIE DOUGH

1 cup (2 sticks) butter, room temperature

1½ cups sugar

3 eggs

¾ cup orange juice concentrate

2 to 3 tsp. orange peel, grated

3⅓ cups flour

1 tsp. salt

1 tsp. baking soda

Preheat the oven to 350°. Mix together the butter and sugar. Add the eggs, orange juice concentrate, and orange zest (if you don't have a zester, use a small-hole cheese grater). Blend in the flour, salt, and baking soda. Use a medium cookie scoop to form the cookies and bake them for 8 to 10 minutes.

FROSTING

¾ cup (1½ sticks) butter, room temperature

4½ cups powdered sugar

2 tsp. orange peel, grated

¼ tsp. salt

½ cup orange juice concentrate

With a hand mixer, blend the butter, powdered sugar, orange peel, salt, and orange juice. Frost cookies to your liking.

Yields 3½ dozen cookies

HOMESTYLE HINT

These cookies are a fun addition to any cookie assortment, and drop cookies are easy to make. I like the way these cookies bake up on a cooking stone, but a regular cookie sheet is just fine.

OREO TRUFFLES

1 pkg. Oreo cookies (36 cookies)

8 oz. cream cheese, softened

1½ cups chocolate wafers (we like to use Merckens)

White chocolate for drizzle

Place the Oreo cookies in a food processor and chop finely. Mix with the softened cream cheese. Shape into balls the diameter of a quarter and chill. Melt the chocolate wafers in a microwave, then roll the cookie balls in the melted chocolate and place on wax paper.

When hardened, melt the white chocolate and drizzle over the truffles.

Yields approximately 25 to 30 truffles

PEANUT BUTTER FINGERS

When we owned the Farmer's Wife, a little bulk food store, bakery, and deli, an employee of ours, Sandy, was always bringing in recipes to try. It was fun to see what she was cooking up. The recipe below is inspired by Sandy, and it should please the peanut butter and chocolate lovers in your household.

BARS

1 cup (2 sticks) butter, room temperature

1 cup white sugar

1 cup Sucanat or brown sugar

3 eggs

1 cup peanut butter

2 cups flour

2 cups oatmeal

1½ tsp. salt

1 tsp. baking soda

1 tsp. vanilla

2 cups semisweet chocolate chips

Preheat the oven to 350°. Beat together the butter, white sugar, and Sucanat or brown sugar. Add the eggs and peanut butter and beat thoroughly. Add the flour, oatmeal, salt, baking soda, and vanilla and stir just until blended. Pour the mixture onto a jelly roll pan and bake for 20 to 25 minutes or until an inserted toothpick comes out clean. Remove from the oven and top with the 2 cups of chocolate chips. Allow to cool for 30 minutes before glazing.

GLAZE

3½ cups powdered sugar

½ cup milk

1 tsp. vanilla

½ cup peanut butter

Coarse sea salt (optional)

With a hand beater, combine the powdered sugar, milk, vanilla, and peanut butter. Drizzle over the cooled "fingers." The chocolate and glaze will blend nicely, creating an attractive marbling effect. Sprinkle on coarse sea salt, if desired, and cut into bars.

Makes 24 bars

PEPPERMINT ANGEL CAKE ROLL

1 (16 oz.) box angel food cake mix
½ gallon peppermint ice cream, softened
Hot fudge (just enough to drizzle—optional)

Preheat the oven to 350°.

Make the cake mix according to the box's directions.

Line a greased sheet pan with parchment paper or wax paper. Grease the paper too. Pour the cake mix onto pan and bake for 15 to 20 minutes.

Cool 4 to 5 minutes and turn onto a clean kitchen towel dusted with powdered sugar. Roll the cake and towel together, starting at a short end. Let cool completely. When cooled, unroll the cake carefully and spread with the ice cream. Reroll and freeze.

Slice and serve. Drizzle with hot fudge if desired.

Serves 10 to 12

ROSEMARY-SPICED BAKED NUTS

2 cups walnut halves

3 cups cashews, unsalted

2 cups whole pecans

2 T. olive oil

¼ cup brown sugar

1 tsp. cayenne pepper

1 T. + 2 tsp. sea salt

½ cup maple syrup

2 T. dried rosemary

Preheat the oven to 275°. Line a jelly roll pan with parchment paper. Place the walnuts, cashews, and pecans in a large bowl. Add the olive oil, brown sugar, cayenne pepper, 1 tablespoon of the sea salt, maple syrup, and rosemary. Stir well. Place on the pan.

Bake for 30 to 35 minutes, stirring every 10 minutes. When the nuts are glazed and golden, remove from the oven. Add the remaining 2 teaspoons of salt and stir well. Allow to cool or serve warm.

Yields 7½ cups

HOMESTYLE HINT

If you allow the nuts to cool before eating, place them on parchment paper on a counter, stirring once to prevent them from sticking together as they cool. Store in a mason jar at room temperature.

SNOW CREAM

This dessert is a special delight our oldest granddaughter likes to make after a snowfall. If you've not tried this dish, do give it a chance. If not for the taste, then how about for the memories it creates with the beloved young people in your life?

2 eggs

1½ cups sugar

1 cup half-and-half

2 cups milk

1 tsp. vanilla

A large bowl of snow

Beat the eggs for 5 minutes. Add the sugar and beat several more minutes to get a nice, fluffy consistency. Slowly add cream and beat again for several minutes. Add the milk and vanilla and beat until integrated.

Stir in the snow by hand until the consistency is like soft serve ice cream. Serve immediately.

Serves 4

SOUR CREAM COFFEE CAKE WITH CRUMB TOPPING

CAKE

- 1 cup sugar
- 1½ cups flour
- ¼ tsp. salt
- 1 tsp. baking powder
- 1 egg
- 1 cup sour cream
- ½ tsp. baking soda, dissolved in a teaspoon of water

CRUMB TOPPING

- ½ cup brown sugar
- 1 T. butter
- 2 tsp. cinnamon

Preheat the oven to 350°. Combine the dry ingredients for the cake. Add eggs and sour cream and beat well. Add the baking soda dissolved in water. Grease a Bundt pan and pour half of the batter into the pan.

Combine the crumb topping ingredients, and add all but 2 tablespoons to the batter. Add the remaining batter and top with the remaining crumb mixture. Bake for 30 minutes or until done. Allow to cool, then invert over a serving plate. The cake should fall out. Cut into slices and serve.

Serves 16

TURTLE CAKE

My sister Rose introduced me to this delicacy. Turtle cake is a treat, but sharing it with Rose made it even sweeter. Sharing food with loved ones somehow enhances the flavor. As we eat together, we are reminded of how truly blessed we are. Remember to see the special people in your life—and the times you spend with them—as gifts from God.

    1 box German chocolate cake mix
    1 (11.75 oz.) jar caramel ice cream topping
    6 oz. chopped pecans

Mix and bake the cake mix according to the package directions. Using the handle of a wooden spoon, poke holes into the baked cake and pour the caramel ice cream topping over it. Add the chopped pecans. When serving, garnish with a scoop of whipped cream.

Serves 16

UPSIDE-DOWN DATE PUDDING

This is a simpler version of traditional date pudding. We like to use this recipe when we are in a hurry and want a nice, quick dessert.

DATE MIXTURE

> 1 cup dates, diced
> 1 cup boiling water
> 1 tsp. baking soda

Mix the ingredients above and allow to cool to lukewarm temperature.

PUDDING MIXTURE

> ½ cup sugar
> ½ cup brown sugar
> 1 egg
> 2 T. butter
> 1½ cups flour
> 1 tsp. salt
> 1 tsp. baking powder

Blend together the sugars, eggs, and butter. Add the remaining dry ingredients, and then stir in the date mixture. Pour into a 9 x 13-inch baking dish.

SAUCE MIXTURE

> 1½ cups brown sugar or ½ cup maple syrup
> 1 T. butter
> 1½ cups boiling water

Preheat the oven to 350°. Combine all ingredients and then pour the sauce over the date mixture and bake for 35 minutes. To serve, cut into small squares, place in a serving dish, and top with whipped cream.

Serves 15

WONDERFUL SIMPLE CARAMELS

2¼ cups brown sugar

1 cup sweetened condensed milk (we suggest Eagle Brand)

1 cup light corn syrup

1 cup (2 sticks) butter

Combine all of the ingredients in a medium saucepan. Bring mixture to a boil, being careful to stir constantly. Boil for 12 minutes. Pour into a greased 9 x 13-inch pan. Cool completely, cut into small pieces, and wrap in waxed paper, twisting the ends. Mmm…good!

Yields 117 1-inch caramels

BONUS
"NATURAL LIVING"
RECIPES

Beef Bone Broth

Deodorant

Fermented Kraut

Foaming Hand Soap

Ever since I sold the Farmer's Wife at the end of 2008, I have been removing synthetic products and chemicals from our household. It has been a very *slow* journey as I educate myself and make changes. Sometimes the changes are slow because I don't know the best place to buy replacement products, such as shampoos and conditioners without unhealthy ingredients. Other times, price is a factor.

The task can make a person weary, because sometimes it seems as if *everything* is bad for us in some way. We can become so discouraged that we don't want to make *any* changes. We are all susceptible to the various marketing ploys and "revolutionary" new research. But I keep going back to what anchors me. I recall how many sick people walked through the doors of the Farmer's Wife, seeking healthy alternatives to various products.

Baby step by baby step, I have moved to a place I feel good about today. We are mortal beings. We will not live on this earth forever. However, I have this inherent, God-given motherly drive to do my best to provide the best possible environment for my husband and children. (I shared a few of the changes I made in my previous book, *A Farmer's Daughter*, along with several recipes for a more toxin-free life.)

BEEF BONE BROTH

Some research suggests that beef bone broth contains minerals that help the digestion process. When our youngest child suffers from some food allergies, I am constantly making food with bone broth—such as vegetables cooked in the broth. I don't know all of the science behind it, but I believe this broth is a key factor in getting him to a good, healthy place.

    3 to 4 lbs. beef bones
    1 large onion
    2 carrots, tops off
    2 stalks celery with celery leaves on
    8 to 12 whole garlic cloves
    2 T. apple cider vinegar (to extract minerals from the bones)

Place all of your ingredients in one or two slow cookers. Cover completely with water. This broth is pungent as it simmers, so I place my cookers in the basement. Set your cooker(s) on low and allow to simmer for 24 to 36 hours.

Cool the broth so you can remove the vegetables and garlic cloves. I divide my broth into 1- or 2-cup servings and freeze for use in soups, pasta, or any other dishes that require broth.

Depending on your slow cooker size, you can get anywhere between 12 to 20 cups

---

HOMESTYLE HINT

A lot of butchers cut off the bones before packaging meat for sale. If you are having beef custom cut, be sure to tell your butcher you want to keep the larger bones when your meat is cut and wrapped. And you can usually buy broth bones (soup bones) in the frozen meat section of your local grocery store. (I often buy three or four pounds of bones at a time and freeze them for later use.)

DEODORANT

Coconut oil liquefies at about 77 degrees, so you must be careful where you store this deodorant, especially in the summer. (My husband took some of it on a flight, and it melted all over his travel bag. He purchased a heat-stable natural deodorant for future flights.)

- 1½ cups organic cornstarch
- 1½ cups baking soda
- 1½ cups organic coconut oil, melted down
- 8 empty deodorant containers (you can wash old ones and reuse them if desired)
- 36 drops essential oil

Combine the cornstarch and baking soda. Melt the coconut oil and mix with the cornstarch/soda mixture. Stir until the dry ingredients dissolve completely. Add the essential oils and pour the mixture into deodorant containers. Allow to set on your counter for several hours until the coconut oil re-hardens.

Yields 6 containers

HOMESTYLE HINT

For the men in your house, you can make this deodorant with masculine scents such as sandalwood, pine, and peppermint/orange citrus.

FERMENTED KRAUT

This simple recipe packs some great probiotics. While researchers are still learning exactly how probiotics work, it's believed that they aid in digestion, helping our bodies absorb maximum nutrients from the foods we eat.

I never imagined I would enjoy kraut as a side dish with my meals, but I feel good about eating it. I believe it helps my body digest food more efficiently and effectively. I started making fermented kraut because it's much cheaper than the probiotics sold at grocery stores and drugstores. In a strange kind of way, fermented kraut has grown on me (and in me).

 2 large cabbage heads, about 32 cups shredded

 2 to 2½ T. sea salt

 1 (2 gallon) clear glass container (e.g., a large punch bowl or crock)

 Crock-Pot liner bags or BPA-free 1-gallon freezer bags to weight the cabbage

Shred the cabbage and place in a clear jar or crock. Sprinkle with the salt and stir. Mash with a wooden spoon and allow to set for 30 minutes. Mash the cabbage again (you want to produce enough liquid to reach the top of the cabbage).

Once the liquid is visible near the top of your container, it is time to weight your cabbage. Fill the bags with water, seal them, and use them to cover the cabbage completely. (I double-bag to protect against leaks.) Place your container in a cool dark cupboard or basement for approximately 2 to 3 weeks. (You basically ignore it this entire time.) Once the fermentation process is complete, divide the kraut into mason jars and refrigerate. (It will keep for up to 6 months.) You can eat 1 or 2 tablespoons with every meal.

Yields approximately 3 quarts

FOAMING HAND SOAP

1 (8 or 10 oz.) empty foam pump container

2 to 3 T. liquid castile soap (I like Doctor Bronner's Lavender)

5 to 7 drops tea tree essential oil. (This oil can kill bacteria and fungi, but it doesn't have the best smell.)

12 to 15 drops of essential oil of your choice (my favorite is clove)

1 tsp. vegetable glycerin

1 cup cold water

In your container, combine the castile soap, tea tree oil, essential oil of your choice, glycerin, and water. Place the top on and give the bottle a few shakes. Experiment with various essential oils to find the scents you like best. I like clove, peppermint, and spearmint. If you're looking for a less-expensive alternative, try citrus oils.

1 container

HOMESTYLE HINT

Look for glycerin in the pharmacy section of your favorite store. However, it's worth shopping around, as glycerin can be pricey at some places (and it really shouldn't be). Also, you can buy foaming soap containers on Amazon.com. I have about 10 of them, which I use over and over. (If you have kids, I recommend plastic bottles. I purchased a glass bottle once, and my kids broke it within a week.) For the sake of efficiency, I make enough soap to fill up all of my bottles at once.

PARTING THOUGHTS FROM DAWN

In our Pinterest and Instagram world, the mere thought of entertaining dinner guests can be overwhelming. I encourage you with this: Don't put the pressure of perfection on yourself.

In fact, I've chosen to forgo Instagram because, as a homeschooling mama, I don't have the time or energy to deal with the pressure that online content can produce. I even limit my Facebook presence because I know how much time and energy *that* site can drain from my days.

I am not saying you must follow my example regarding social media. I'm simply sharing what I'm doing to ensure I'm fully present for my family. God has placed creativity in me, and this helps me cook and entertain creatively without the bombardment of mass media.

Is my house "Pinterest Perfect"? No. But I've crafted a place we all love to come home to. I encourage you to find inspiration from your friends and relatives and the creativity they demonstrate. Be blessed and inspired by them but not pressured to be them.

Further, look at the sunrise God paints for you tomorrow morning. Listen to the words your children say. I am blown away, for example, by what my two-year-old already knows and expresses in his own unique way. His words make us laugh, and they are the thumbprints of God. Be blessed by moments with your family. Don't compare your family with someone else's. Be thankful for what you have, and let it move you to worship the Creator of all these good things, the things we should savor in our lives.

In this season of my life, I have drastically scaled down my entertaining. I don't focus on having it all: beautifully crafted tablescapes, bang-up meals, *and* artistically arranged dessert buffets anymore. When I am hosting a meal, I strive to focus on *one* main thing, not three or four. And I focus on what is important to me rather than being pressured by others' expectations.

It's good to be stretched—to grow spiritually and in other ways too. I believe God calls us to do that, but we also need rest and stability in our lives. We all live with some pressure, but the balance comes between our striving to be the best we can be while still accepting the constraints of reality.

We must decide what is truly important to us and then press in to who we are and what we have to offer the world. Ultimately, I encourage you to let your love for your family and your guests shine the brightest. And if you're just not feeling the love, ask God to fill your soul with love. You'll be amazed at how He will change you, even before you hear that first knock at your door.

RECIPE INDEX